Experienced Career Professionals Endorse
Job Search Work Teams

"The Job Search Work Team is one of most successful — and by far the most transformational — innovation in the history of career transition services. Job hunters embrace the experience and get jobs faster."

Steve Harrison, Co-founder and Chairman of Lee Hecht Harrison, a 300-office global career services company, 35 years experience in career work

"Orville's book is a must read for anyone who wants to land a new job quickly. As a team facilitator, I've discovered how team members flourish in this structure, and often say that the team meetings are the highlight of their week. This book makes a critical component of job searching smart, easy and accessible."

Jean Baur, 19 years in career work in Rhode Island and New Jersey, Job Search Work Team (JSWT) leader for 15 years.

"If you are supporting job seekers in church or community based job help groups, this practical how-to manual should be your constant companion. Pierson is nationally known for innovative search principles. He has engineered, perfected and tested this unique search strategy that has shortened thousands of job searches and decreased untold numbers of failed attempts. An invaluable resource!"

Edward J. DeVries, Ph.D., Career Coach in Illinois and Tennessee for 20 years, 9 years as a JSWT leader

"The JSWT methodology is a key component in leading my clients down the path of successful transition. The structure of the meetings help team members stay focused on achieving their goals. The process invites team members to create a true team environment where everyone "owns" each others' searches - and networking occurs as a natural outcome."

Deborah Krawiec, Connecticut, 21 years in career consulting, 17 years experience with JSWTs

"Undoubtedly, the two most effective job search strategies involve networking and Job Search Work Teams. Orville's book, *Highly Effective Networking* so effectively addressed the former and now he tackles the second. I can attest firsthand to the advantages and effectiveness of both books. Orville articulates what you need to do – and how and why."

Joe Ciola, 12 years as JSWT facilitator and leadership coach in California

"As a Career Coach, I worked closely with Orville in the implementation of Job Search Work Teams (JSWTs) at Lee Hecht Harrison. I witnessed firsthand the profound benefit that team membership provides to a job seeker.

Orville's latest book, *Team Up!* intimately describes the philosophies and inner workings of JSWTs, enabling individual job seekers to form their own teams and reap the benefits of accountability, planning, self-knowledge and greater potential for success. Quite frankly, his work is genius."

Andrew Johnson, California, 20 years of JSWT experience, including seven at a major university. 21 years in career work, plus 12 as an executive recruiter

"*Team Up!* is a great guide to forming and running a job search group, whether you are a professional career coach or a layperson working to help people in a community organization. Orville offers practical advice on how to form, grow and manage the work team. In a period of ongoing change in the economy, industries and companies, it is helpful to have a group of peers who are in the market to provide real-time insights into what they find works. The work team, as envisioned by Orville, provides the mechanism for this."

Jay Colan, New York City, 24 years experience in career work, 14 years experience with JSWTs

"Participation on a team improves an individual's success rate and creates a workplace structure complete with a leader, peers, best practices, and metrics for measuring job search effectiveness."

Grace M. Totoro, Florida, Career & Life Strategy Coach and JSWT leader, both 15 years

"The unity of the team inspires the members to execute their job searches in a productive and professional manner. The genius of Pierson's JSWT is the driving force of 12 members intensely focused for two hours on connecting themselves to work. What gets measured gets done. JSWT is a sanctuary for rebuilding careers. It is personal and it is successful. In the past 30 months at St. Patrick's, 41 job offers were accepted by members of the JSWT."

Ed McEneney, 20 years in career work, JSWT leader for 14 years

"Teams have transformed the process for job searchers who participate in them. The benefits are numerous: Members feel they're not alone; the metrics provide clarity for their actions; productivity is increased; sharing knowledge and experience is the order of the day so everyone improves their game. People need structure and discipline — especially during periods of unemployment — and Orville's process answers that critical need."

Claudia Gentner, 25 years working with job seekers, executive positions at three career services firms, currently leading a church-sponsored JSWT

Team Up!

Find a Better Job Faster with
a Job Search Work Team

The Proven Program Used by 300 Career

Coaches and Thousands of Job Hunters

at the World's Leading Career Company

Version 5.0

By Orville Pierson

www.highlyeffectivejobsearch.com

ISBN: 0615924883
ISBN-13: 978-0615924885
LCCN: 2013956299

Highly Effective Job Search
Northampton, Massachusetts

This publication is designed to provide accurate and authoritative information on the subjects covered.
It is sold with the understanding that neither the publisher nor the author is engaged in rendering legal,
accounting, or other professional services. If legal or other expert assistance is required, the services of
a competent professional should be sought.

Contents

This book will show you a new and better way to do job hunting, as a member of a supportive and productive team. In this introductory chapter, I'll outline the whole book for you. I'll give you an overview of how it all works – and the elements you can use to create your own personal job hunting program.

These teams have been used by thousands of job hunters for over 20 years and included in programs offered by nonprofits, religious communities, educational institutions and a global outplacement firm. Studies show that they provide numerous advantages. In this chapter, I'll define the teams and show you the evidence that they make job hunting more effective, more comfortable and faster.

Before you have a job offer — or even an interview — how do you know whether your job search is effective? If it is, you should do more of the same. But if it's not, you should start doing things differently right now. In this chapter, I'll give you some simple progress measurements that will tell you how well — and how fast — your job search is moving.

In the last 20 years, job hunting has changed dramatically. It's not just about the Internet; it's also about how job hunters can collaborate to get the work done better. I'll tell you about job search programs over the years, so you can see what worked, what didn't, and why. And you'll see exactly how the newer methods make it all go better.

5. The Job Search Work Team Manual

These 25 pages tell you everything you need to know to join a team, serve as a leader of a team or start a new team.

6. The Job Search Work Team Toolkit

Here are samples of the tools you'll need for your team, and instructions on using each. All of these are downloadable from my website, www.highlyeffectivejobsearch.com, free of charge.

7. Your Personal Job Hunting Program

Now that you understand teams and tools, I'll show you a job search skills curriculum. And I'll outline your options for combining the team, the tools and the curriculum into a powerful personal job hunting program, one you can use in your current job search and in any future job hunting as well.

A Note to Career Professionals

Research Citations

Acknowledgements

About the Author

Orville Pierson is a top expert in job search assistance. He is the author of *The Unwritten Rules of the Highly Effective Job Search* (McGraw-Hill) and *Highly Effective Networking: Meet the Right People and Get a Great Job* (Career Press).

Assisted over a million job hunters

He served for 19 years as Corporate Director of Program Design at the headquarters of Lee Hecht Harrison (LHH), a global career services company with 300 offices worldwide. He led a design team that created job-hunting programs used to assist over a million job hunters in finding good new jobs.

Trained hundreds of career coaches

In that role, Mr. Pierson created the overall LHH job-search curriculum and was the primary or sole author of dozens of privately published LHH books, manuals and websites. He created LHH's ground breaking Job Search Work Team (JSWT) program and certified leaders and master facilitators. He also designed a wide range of training materials for LHH's staff and trained hundreds of career coaches worldwide.

Talks and trainings for universities, businesses, and career professionals

Mr. Pierson has been in the career services field since 1977 as a program designer, as well as a trainer, coach and consultant to hundreds of private clients. He has spoken at universities and business schools, as well as to groups of executives, human resources professionals, and college career professionals. He has appeared on radio and TV and has been featured in many articles, ranging from the NACE Journal to Forbes.com to general audience publications. His education includes a BA from Yale University and training in career-related psychological instruments.

For complete information on Mr. Pierson's experience, please see his LinkedIn profile or his website, www.highlyeffectivejobsearch.com.

Preface

to the Fifth Edition (version 5.0) of the
Job Search Work Team (JSWT) Manual

This book is the first comprehensive Job Search Work Team manual available to the general public. I wrote the original manual for JSWTs in 1992 exclusively for career professionals at Lee Hecht Harrison (LHH), currently a 300–office global career services company.

As the company gained experience with JSWTs, I wrote a second edition in 1994 and a third in 1998. All of these manuals were designed to teach career professionals how to lead teams. Those coaches then instructed job hunters in the use of the teams.

The 2006 JSWT manual, published as a Special Section in my book, *The Unwritten Rules of the Highly Effective Job Search*, was the first version written especially for teams led by job hunters rather than career consultants. Under a licensing agreement with LHH, it incorporated the essential elements of the first three editions. But because it was only a single chapter, it was not as comprehensive as earlier editions.

In the years following that publication, JSWTs were adopted by job search assistance programs sponsored by religious communities and nonprofit organizations. Some of those have a paid professional staff. In others, the teams are led by volunteer workers or by the job hunters themselves.

This book is the fifth edition (version 5.0) of the JSWT manual. It is the most comprehensive ever written, and includes new insights from recent experience. It incorporates all the benefits of over 20 years of team experience, and it can be used by member-led or professionally led teams. I wrote it in the hope and expectation of making this proven program available to an even broader general audience.

May it help many, many job hunters find great new jobs.

Orville Pierson

CHAPTER ONE

A Better Way To Do Job Hunting

Most people would say that I'm a consultant, author and speaker — and I am. I've advised and coached job hunters for over 35 years. I've trained career professionals in how to coach job hunters for over 25 years. I've consulted with managers of job search assistance programs. I've written books. And I've spoken to audiences large and small.

But what most people don't notice is that I'm primarily a program designer. My most important work has been designing programs to help job hunters conduct job searches that are more comfortable, more effective and faster than those using traditional methods. The Job Search Work Team (JSWT) program, the subject of this book, is undoubtedly the best program I ever designed.

This book will *not* tell you how to do all the tasks of a job search, like planning, resume writing, networking, interviewing, using the Internet and all the rest. There are hundreds of books available on those topics, including two of mine.

Instead, this book introduces you to a new way of doing job hunting––as a member of a highly supportive and unusually productive team. It tells you everything you need to know to join, start, or lead such a team — and make that team part of your personal job hunting program.

I'll begin in Chapter 2 by giving you a brief explanation of what the Job Search Work Team is. I know that the name is a bit long, but it carries an important message. I chose the name many years ago when I was working exclusively with people who lost their jobs in layoffs.

As you may know, getting hit by a layoff is not a pleasant experience. It's a shock, and one that can create a feeling of helplessness. You did your best at work and made real contributions, but you were let go anyway, in spite of your best efforts. It can make you feel powerless.

But while you might feel powerless in avoiding a layoff, you are definitely not powerless about getting a new job. You don't need to just sit and wait for employers to respond to your resume. You have the power to conduct a strong, proactive search. You can plan and manage it, using methods proven to be effective. And you can diligently do the required work, day after day, until you succeed.

With all that in mind, I called the teams Job Search *Work* Teams to remind people who were laid off that there is a great deal of important work to be done in job hunting. I also wanted to remind them to approach that work in the same professional way that they always manage work projects. And remind them that working as part of a team is a great way to complete any project.

In Chapter 2, then, I'll start with a definition of these teams. I'll show you the evidence that doing your job hunting on a team is more effective, more comfortable and faster than doing it alone. I have included several studies as well as some strong anecdotal evidence.

One of the reasons that these particular teams are so effective is that team members use numerical progress measurements. As you know, it's difficult to manage any project without some kind of objective progress measurements. The job search project is no exception.

How can you tell if you're making progress?

Before you have a job offer, or even an interview, how can you tell if you're making progress in your job search? If you're making good progress, you should continue to do more of what you have been doing. On the other hand, if you're not making any progress, you should try some different methods.

But if you don't know whether you're making progress or not, you have a serious problem. It's like swimming in molasses at midnight. You're not sure which way you're heading, and you don't know if you're getting anywhere. It's discouraging.

So in Chapter 3, I'll tell you about a simple system of numerical progress tracking. I'll tell you where it came from and why it's useful. These measurements will make your search more effective whether you join a team or not. But if you use the measurements in a supportive peer group like a Job Search Work Team, you can also get some objective opinions on what the numbers mean for your search––and what you should do next.

The job search revolution

Then, in Chapter 4, I'll tell you about the job search revolution. It's partly about using the Internet, of course. But you might be surprised to find out that the Internet is not the central factor. I'll show you how job hunting has changed over the years, so you can see whether your methods are the most effective and up-to-date. Or whether there are some better methods that you should try.

You'll learn exactly how to create and maintain a highly effective and very comfortable team.

> *If you're not making any progress, you should try some different methods.*

I'll include the teams in that discussion, of course. But I'll also provide some information on job search assistance program design, information that will enable you to put together a personal job hunting program, the one that's best for you.

In Chapter 5, I'll give you the best JSWT manual ever written. Chapters 2, 3 and 4 are about the "what" and the "why" of teams. Chapters 5 is the "how-to-do-it" part, where you'll learn exactly how to create and maintain a highly effective and very comfortable team.

If you decide to create a new team, the manual in Chapter 5 will tell you everything you need to know in order to do that. If you decide to join an existing member–led team, the manual will explain how they work. In a team like that, it's possible that you will be a leader as well as a member, so I'll tell you how that's done, too. And if you're planning to join a professionally led team, Chapter 5 will tell you what to expect and how to behave so that the team works well for everyone, including you.

There are several productivity tools that are useful in job hunting and particularly useful in the teams. In Chapter 6, I'll give you a sample copy of each of those and tell you how you can download additional free copies from my website. And of course, I'll explain each of them, and tell you exactly how and when they're used.

Finally, in Chapter 7, I'll show you a job search skills curriculum, a list of the subjects taught in any good job hunting course. If there are skills you'd like to improve, I'll tell you how you can do that. And I'll show you how to put that skills curriculum together with everything we discussed in the book, to create a personal job hunting program for yourself –– one that's likely to get you into a great new job faster.

If you're a career professional who is not a job hunter, I'm happy to have you reading this book too. I've included a note for you at the end. In the meantime, I hope you'll excuse me for addressing everything directly to the job hunters. But when they understand it all, your job in a team-based program will be much easier.

Of course, that's true of member-led teams, too. When everyone has read this book, those teams go smoothly and very effectively. So let's get started by defining the teams and looking at the evidence of their effectiveness.

CHAPTER TWO

Job Search Work Teams: A Proven Method

Before you picked up this book, you already knew that job search can be difficult. It can be tough in a good job market. In a bad job market, it can be brutal.

Job search is different from your usual work. You might be accustomed to working in an organization where you have colleagues, resources and established ways of getting the work done. But in job search, you're completely on your own, working solo on a difficult project.

As a job hunter, you're constantly faced with the "black hole" of job hunting: you complete applications, post resumes and make contacts, but get no response at all. When there is a response, it's usually a rejection – and you may get dozens and dozens of them. The job of job hunting might be a job you're not interested in or not suited for. But if you're unemployed, it's the only job you have.

I wish I could tell you that Job Search Work Teams immediately eliminate all of these difficulties and provide instant success in job hunting. Unfortunately, there is no magic solution in job search. It requires hard work and a sustained effort.

More comfortable
More effective
Faster

But here's the good news: there is no doubt that these teams make job hunting more comfortable and more effective for the vast majority of people who use them. And of course, when you're more effective, you get things done faster and you get better results.

This isn't just my opinion. The team process has been tested and refined for over 20 years. Studies have been done. There is solid evidence that members of Job Search Work Teams are more positive and more effective than solo job hunters. Best of all, there is evidence that team members are likely to find jobs faster than non-team members.

In this chapter, you'll see the evidence that shows how very effective these teams are. But let's begin with a brief definition.

A Job Search Work Team is a group of 6 to 12 job hunters that meets for up to two hours each week. The focus of the meetings is job search effectiveness. Each team member gives a brief report on their progress, using a simple numerical progress tracking system that I'll describe in the next chapter. Then team members list job hunting problems and issues that have come up during the week. The team discusses these to enumerate options and find solutions.

Each week, members get a little better at job hunting. Over time, they get a lot better — unless of course they find a great new job first.

The team is an ongoing group. As members find jobs, they are replaced by new members. So less experienced job hunters learn from those with more experience. And new members bring fresh perspectives and additional resources.

The team provides networking support, personal support, and accountability. All discussions are positive and effectiveness-oriented. Each member is responsible for their own search, but collaboration helps everyone conduct a stronger search. No one is ever required to share information or contacts, but team members often do, because networking is easier as people get to know each other.

But here's the most important thing you need to know about Job Search Work Teams: team

The Job Search Work Team (JSWT)

- Weekly meetings of 6 to 12 job hunters

- Networking, support and accountability

- Team members value and enjoy the process

- "It kept me going."

"JSWTs are the most successful innovation in the history of career transition services."

Steve Harrison, Co-founder and Chairman of Lee Hecht Harrison

members *like* them. After they find a job, they will usually tell you that the team was a major contributor to their success. And they often say, "It kept me going, even when things were tough."

JSWTs are not difficult to form and conduct. Whether you want to join an existing team or start a new one, this book will show you how to do it and provide you with everything you need to succeed.

JSWTs get results: team members found jobs 20% faster

I first instituted Job Search Work Teams at Lee Hecht Harrison (LHH), a career services company, in 1992. The company then had fewer than 100 offices, but it grew rapidly to become the 300-office global company that it is today. Job Search Work Teams were part of that success.

When JSWTs had been introduced in half of the company's offices, the other half was still using traditional job search assistance methods. At that time, LHH compared the time-to-placement in team offices with non-team offices. People in the offices with teams found jobs 20% faster. And of course, the job hunters in the non-team offices were already doing well, since they were working

Job Search Work Teams Get Results

- Proven successful for over 20 years with thousands of job hunters

- Team members found jobs 20% faster than non-team members

- Studies document JSWT effectiveness

under the guidance of highly experienced career professionals.

That 20% is particularly significant to unemployed job hunters. It shortens a five-month job search to a four-month search. That's a full month's salary.

LHH has used Job Search Work Teams for over 20 years, and now offers several different versions of them. Thousands and thousands of job hunters have found good new jobs using the team program. Steve Harrison, LHH's co-founder and Chairman, called JSWTs "the most successful — and by far the most transformational — innovation in the history of career transition services."

LHH routinely uses written service evaluations. Over the years, team members consistently reported that teams were one of the most valuable elements of their job search assistance program. And they reported enjoying the team experience.

Job Clubs and Job Search Work Teams

The original team-based job search assistance program was called "Job Club." It was created many years before JSWTs by a behavioral psychologist, Dr. Nathan Azrin. The U.S. Department of Labor conducted control–group studies that

compared Job Clubs to traditional job search assistance methods. Job Club members found jobs in one-third the time of job hunters using traditional methods.

There is a major, central similarity between the two processes: Job Club and Job Search Work Team members both use a defined system of numerical progress tracking in a supportive, task–oriented peer group setting. I see that as a central factor in the success of both — and the main reason why both programs get people into new jobs faster.

There are also some differences between the two. Job Clubs were designed for hourly workers, while Job Search Work Teams are designed for salaried workers ranging from entry level to experienced managers, professionals and executives. So while they have some central similarities, the two programs are certainly not identical.

Since JSWTs got started in the early 1990s, there have been three formal studies of the effectiveness of this kind of program. Two of those were specifically on JSWTs. Here are brief summaries of all three:

Research on job clubs for salaried professionals finds them effective

The success of the original Job Clubs with hourly workers raised the question of whether that kind of "club" activity would increase the effectiveness of salaried job hunters. Research completed by Lola Mae Coxford in 1998 for her PhD at Clare-

An unpublished 2003 study of JSWTs demonstrates their effectiveness

Later research focused specifically on Job Search Work Teams. A qualitative study of JSWTs was completed by Melanie Parkin in 2003 for a Master of Science degree at the London School of Economics and Political Science.

Job Search Work Teams offer networking benefits and members better understand job search.

mont Graduate University evaluated job clubs for salaried professional workers.

Her study found that the job clubs increased "job-seeking behaviors" and "motivated job seekers to be persistent in their efforts." She also found that job club members assisted each other in becoming "sources of reinforcement, feedback and mutual critique as they shared sources of information and stories of success."

This research concluded that JSWTs displayed "a mix of information-sharing, motivation, and support qualities" as well as "confidence-building factors such as efficacy." The study also demonstrated that the JSWTs supported individual accountability in job hunting.

A 2009 study published by the Journal of Employment Counseling documents benefits of JSWTs

This qualitative study compared JSWT members to job hunters using only traditional methods. Published in 2009 by Dr. Christopher Kondo, it gave LHH a fictional name, "Walsh and Brown." JSWTs were called job clubs. Team members were called "Clubbers" and non-team members were called "Soloists." He also referred to them as "tortoises" and "hares," since the team members' steady, methodical approach won the race. A complete citation for this study is on page 111.

Dr. Kondo's research found numerous benefits of teams as well as a number of positive attributes of "Clubbers" (e.g., they worked harder) and a number of negative attributes of "Soloists" (e.g., they were frustrated or bewildered by job search). The key findings are summarized below.

In-depth interviews with team members confirmed that JSWTs offered:

- a useful learning experience

- social and emotional support

- networking benefits

Compared to non-team job hunters, JSWT members:

- better understood job search

- better accepted accountability for the search project

- displayed a more positive attitude

- devoted double the weekly hours to job hunting

You may have noticed that these research studies mention things like "increasing job-seeking behavior," "motivation" and the number of hours devoted to job hunting. In the next chapter, we'll take a closer look at why those things are so important to job hunting success.

CHAPTER THREE

Numerical Progress Tracking: An Essential Part of Effective Job Search

One of my favorite activities is working with job hunters, career professionals, and human resources managers on the topic of job search assistance. I've done this for many years, as a speaker and workshop leader, with groups ranging from a half dozen to 200 or more.

For the last 20 years, there is one question that I have often asked these groups:

"How many hours per week does the average unemployed job hunter spend looking for a new job?"

The answers I get nearly always range from two or three hours per week to 20 hours per week.

Now and then, someone will suggest that job hunters put in 40 hours or more. When that happens, I remind them that, "I'm talking about the average job hunter, not you."

"Oh," they say, and then they give me a number between two and 20 hours.

Or I'll say, "I'm not talking about what job hunters *should* do, I'm talking about what they actually do." And again the number drops to something below 20. I've discovered that it's very rare that someone believes that the average job hunter puts in a lot of hours.

Formal studies say the same thing. A U.S. Department of Labor study showed that two thirds of job hunters reported working on job search five hours per week or less. I have seen a number of more recent university studies, all with similar results, ranging as low as 41 minutes per day.

Job search intensity is essential to success

The professors of psychology, sociology and economics who do these studies call it "job search intensity." Numerous studies clearly show that higher intensity brings better results, and achieves them more quickly. But the studies also show that most job hunters do not devote enough time to job search. I've listed several of these studies on page 111 in case you want to take a look.

So it seems that pretty much everyone agrees that unemployed job hunters do not devote a great deal of time to their job searches, even though they know it's important. On the surface, this makes very little sense. They need a job. They probably need the money. So those low numbers raise another more important question, one that I always ask as a follow-up:

"Why do job hunters have such low productivity in job search?"

I always get the same list of answers for that question, too. I know that these answers are correct, because I've observed them myself in many, many job hunters over the 35 years that I've been doing job search assistance. Job hunters often have low productivity, but it's not because they're lazy. There are some very understandable reasons for it.

Here are six of the most important reasons for low productivity in job hunting, reasons that I've heard repeatedly over the years:

1. Working solo, with no colleagues or organizational resources

In your normal work projects, you work as part of an organization, inside of an established structure. You work with other people, informally or in formal groups or teams. There is a manager who organizes the work, answers questions, and maybe helps to solve problems. There are established work hours and you usually have a well-equipped workplace, created for the kind of work that you do.

As a job hunter, you typically have none of these supports. You're on your own. You're all alone. And that's usually a barrier to productivity. It's harder to get the work done.

2. Lack of objectivity

Job hunting is personal. It's about finding the work that fits with your life. It's about describing your strengths––and sometimes your weaknesses as well––to a lot of people, some of them complete strangers. It's about finding your way through a complex communications project that you may find uncomfortable. It can be hard to stay objective.

Normal work situations are much less personal, and you usually have colleagues to discuss your ideas with, so that you stay objective and realistic.

Job hunters usually don't have those advantages, so sometimes it's difficult for them to chart the best course for themselves. Then they might be less effective.

3. Limited experience in job search

Some people are fortunate enough to go for many years without having to conduct a job search. But even if you have changed jobs often, you have very limited experience in job hunting. And each time you conduct a new job search, both your work experience and the job market are different from the previous time, so the search is different too.

This means that job hunters are managing a project that they may not understand very well. This is complicated by the fact that there are thousands of books and websites on how to do job hunting. Some of them are excellent. But some of them offer advice that simply doesn't work. Without enough experience, it can be hard to tell the difference and select reliable sources of advice.

As a result, job hunters are sometimes not sure how best to proceed. They simply don't know how to do this job. But choosing the right course of action is critical to success. If what you're doing is effective, you should do more of it. If what you're doing is ineffective, you should stop doing it. But if you have no good way to tell the difference between the two, that's a serious problem — and a significant obstacle to productivity.

4. Skills mismatch

Even when job hunters clearly understand what needs to be done, they may not have enough of the required skills. Job hunting is a work project that requires a certain set of skills. Some of the required skills may not be your areas of greatest strength.

You may have seen the same thing at work. Sometimes employees are assigned to projects that do not align with their skills. With time, effort and assistance, their skills improve. But at the outset, the result is usually low productivity, a bit of a struggle to get the job done.

This, of course, happens all the time in job hunting.

5. Low interest in required tasks

Even when you have the skills required to do job hunting, you may not have a lot of interest in exercising those skills. Once again, you can see this in the workplace. Sometimes someone has a job that they just plain don't like. They would rather avoid it, and when possible, they do. So achieving reasonable productivity is difficult.

6. Rejection, discouragement, and inactivity

This is the big one.

It's mentioned every time I ask about barriers to productivity in the job search project. It might be as important as all of the others put together.

Rejection is common in job hunting. It happens all the time. Job hunters usually get a lot of rejections before they get that one big "Yes!" And they often have the "black hole" experience — no response at all.

When faced with repeated rejections — rejections that can feel very personal — normal human beings become discouraged, or even a bit depressed. Most people don't wake up in the morning and think, "Wow! I just can't wait to go out and get rejected a few more times." We'd all rather avoid that kind of thing as much as possible.

This repeated rejection is a central issue in job search. There is very little positive reinforcement along the way to success. It's rejection, rejection, rejection, rejection, rejection, rejection, rejection, rejection and more rejection. Then success!

Job hunters often become discouraged during those extended periods of rejection. It's hard to keep going when nothing seems to be working. Their activity level drops. They don't do as much as they should. Their effectiveness suffers.

JSWTs help you overcome all six barriers to productivity

The reason I took the time to tell you about these barriers to productivity in such detail is because I want to inoculate you against them. When you're aware of them, you can keep an eye on them. And there are things you can do about them. I designed the teams specifically to help people get past these barriers and conduct a highly effective job search.

JSWTs immediately overcome the first three barriers. When you're on a team, you are not working solo. Your teammates help you maintain objectivity. And team members pool their experience and knowledge as the group becomes an advisory panel for each individual.

The second three barriers — skills mismatch, low interest, and rejection — all reduce the level of effective job search activity. That's why we see such low levels of "job search intensity" in all of the studies.

So Job Search Work Teams are designed to support job hunters in maintaining a reasonable level of effective activity every week, week after week, in spite of the barriers. One of the ways the teams accomplish this is by using progress measurements.

Progress measurements: the key to productivity in job search

Project managers often say, "What gets measured gets managed." That's certainly true in job search. You need a way to tell whether your activity level, your job search intensity, is high enough. And you need measurements that show you how to best allocate your efforts, and how to best manage the search project.

With the right progress measurements, you can see yourself making steady progress in productive directions, so you're better able to hang in and keep going. You have "wins" every week. Things to celebrate. Things to keep you motivated.

You also have more confidence in the methods you're using, because you can see them producing the intermediate results that you know will take you to the ultimate goal of landing a great new job. Measurements also show you *which* of your activities are working best, so you can focus your efforts on the methods that are the most productive for you.

So let's take a look at which progress measurements are most important in the job hunting project.

We need a better measurement than "hours worked"

We've seen how the number of hours you spend in job hunting each week is a useful basic measure of job search intensity, the intensity that experts agree is essential to success. It's the measurement that researchers usually use in doing studies on job search, because it's simple and easy to use. And it's a basic indicator of job search productivity. After all, you can't accomplish much in only 41 minutes a day.

But unless you know how many hours a successful job search takes, counting your weekly hours doesn't tell you if you're making progress towards your goal. The dilemma is that no one knows how many hours a successful job search takes. It varies from person to person and job market to job market. And, of course, it depends on what you do with those hours.

Progress measurements provide answers to three central job hunting questions:

1. Before you have a job offer — or even an interview — how do you know if you're making progress in your job search?

2. Which of your job hunting activities produce the most progress?

3. How much progress did you make this week?

*Job hunters often have low productivity,
but it's not because they're lazy.*

So in job hunting, just like in other work projects, we need better progress measurements than "hours worked." We need measurements that are related to achieving the goal of finding a great new job in a reasonable time.

I noticed this problem of job hunting progress measurements back in 1991. I did some informal research to gather the data I needed to put together a progress measurement system that's practical and effective without being too complex. I'll walk you through what I did, so you can see where the measurements come from and why they're so important.

Decision Maker Conversations: The #1 Progress Measurement

The single most important measure of progress in job hunting is the total number of Decision Makers you have talked to. After all, talking to Decision Makers, the people who could be your next boss, is the most essential step in being hired. So the average number of Decision Makers that job hunters talk to is a useful central performance benchmark in job search. You can use that benchmark number to gauge your progress toward your new job. And your "velocity," how fast you're moving toward that goal.

Yes, I know that it's not quite that simple. You might not be the average job hunter. Job hunting is different for different people. And all Decision Maker "talks" are not the same. Let's take a look at those issues, starting with the last one.

The one thing that every job hunter must do in order to get hired is to have a talk with the Decision Maker who will be their next boss. If that Decision Maker is known to have a job opening and you are seen as a candidate for that opening, then the talk is called a job interview.

However, we all know that 50% to 75% of job hunters find their job through informal networking rather than formal means like Internet job postings or recruiters. When you're networking for a job, it's sometimes hard to tell what's an interview and what isn't.

Suppose, for instance, that you have lunch with a Decision Maker today. As far as you know, that Decision Maker has no job opening. But you have a great talk, covering some of the things that the Decision Maker does and covering some of your skills and experience.

Then suppose that three weeks later (or even three months later), that same Decision Maker has a job opening and invites you to stop by and discuss it. Is that discussion your first interview or your second interview?

In retrospect, it surely looks like the original lunch was actually your first interview. You passed that test and have now made it to the second interview stage. If you did well enough at the lunch, it's even possible that the Decision Maker will now hire you without posting the job or considering other candidates. Networking works like that sometimes.

And what if your initial meeting with the Decision Maker was for just a few minutes, standing in the hallway rather than sitting down for lunch? I think that's still a valuable step towards a new job. In that meeting, you become a real person rather than a resume in a database that the Decision Maker may never use. After all, people hire people, not resumes. And if you were introduced to the Decision Maker by someone they know and trust, so much the better.

25

The average job hunter talks to 25 different Decision Makers on the way to being hired by one of them.

Based on all this, it seemed to me that the total number of Decision Makers a job hunter spoke with would be a useful progress measurement. I chose the number of Decision Makers rather than the number of job interviews for two reasons. First, as we just saw, when you're networking, it's sometimes difficult to tell what's an interview and what's not.

But even more important, you can't control how many interviews you get. If a Decision Maker finds out about you and invites you to an interview, that's great. But the Decision Maker controls it, not you. On the other hand, informal discussions are completely under your control. And some of them turn into formal interviews that produce job offers.

In the end, it doesn't really matter whether you got to talk to a Decision Maker because you responded to a posting, connected with a recruiter or networked for an introduction. Each of those routes has its pros and cons. What matters is that you've met a Decision Maker and are talking to them.

Most job hunters are not hired by the first Decision Maker they talk to — even if that talk is a job interview. Most job hunters need to combine informal networking with formal search methods to make contact with numerous Decision Makers.

How many different Decision Makers do successful job hunters talk to on their way to a great new job? If you know, you can use that number as a way to gauge your rate of progress and focus your efforts.

Three studies, with hundreds of job hunters

So I did my own informal study to determine the average number of Decision Makers that job hunters talk to in order to get a job. I was fortunate to be employed at Lee Hecht Harrison where I had dozens of career consultants to assist me in collecting data from hundreds of job hunters who tracked their activity levels. Over time, I did three different studies, two at LHH and one previous to that. All three produced very similar results.

In the third study, I collected activity data from 168 job hunters. I found that, on average, they talked to 22 different Decision Makers on the way to being hired by one of them. I did not distinguish between formal interviews and informal networking contacts. Nor did I require any particular length of conversation. I simply counted how many different Decision Makers the job hunter spoke to.

I defined "Decision Maker" as the person who could be the job hunter's next boss, or anyone above that level, whether they professed to have an opening or not.

25 Decision Makers

In a previous similar study, the number was 28. Since the original number was also in the mid-20s, I decided to use 25 as the benchmark.

Of course, there were a few job hunters who were hired by the very first Decision Maker they spoke with. At the other extreme, there was one job hunter who spoke to 124 different Decision Makers before being hired by one of them.

What you're doing with these informal conversations is getting on the Decision Maker's "candidate list." That list might be written somewhere, or it might simply be a mental list. Then, when the day comes that the Decision Maker decides to hire someone, you're already on the list.

The more Decision Maker lists you're on, the more likely that one of them will need to hire someone tomorrow. When you're on enough Decision Maker lists, the odds tip in your favor. One of them interviews you and makes an offer that you happily accept. How many is "enough?" Based on the studies, that number is 25.

Regular follow-up with Decision Makers shortens your search.

The most effective job hunters do eight times more follow-up than the least effective.

That average number includes those lucky job hunters who leaped directly into a formal job interview because they found the right posting or connected with the right recruiter. Once again, we're not concerned with how you got there. We're simply counting how many times you succeeded in talking with one of the right Decision Makers.

If you're looking for an executive-level job that pays in the $150K to $500K range, the study says that your Decision Maker number is 35, not 25. If you're a recent graduate looking for your first professional job, I suspect that your Decision Maker number is more like 15, but I have not yet done a study on that.

The Dreaded Bottom Quarter

Here is another interesting fact that emerged from my third informal study. The overall average number of Decision Makers was 25. But the job hunters in the bottom quarter of the study, the quarter where we found that guy who talked to

Informal discussions are completely under your control. And some of them turn into job offers.

124 Decision Makers, averaged 50. So you definitely don't want to be in that bottom quarter.

To do better than that, you need to pay particular attention to follow-up with Decision Makers, since the study also showed that the bottom quarter very seriously neglected that. The top quarter did eight times more follow-up than the bottom quarter.

It's not surprising that failure to follow-up with Decision Makers is associated with a longer job search. Here's how that works: Suppose you talk to a Decision Maker and tell them how very interested you are in working for them. And suppose that you then never contact them again. What will they think?

I see only two possibilities: They think that you weren't really interested. Or they think that you found another job. Either way, they'll probably forget all about you in a month or so. Or if they remember you, they won't bother to call you.

Then you've lost that Decision Maker as a prospective employer and need to replace them with another one. Finding a new Decision Maker is more difficult and more time-consuming than following up with the original one. So follow-up

is essential, and tracking that follow-up is an important progress measurement, along with tracking your initial contacts with Decision Makers.

Your Project Plan

Of course, it's not enough to talk to a whole lot of Decision Makers. You also need to be sure you're talking to the *right* Decision Makers, the ones that are most likely to hire someone like you for a really good job. And you need to talk to them in the right way, providing the information that's most likely to get them to see you as a strong candidate.

The best way to do this is to have a good solid Project Plan for your job search. That Project Plan should include three parts: First, it should define your Professional Objective, the cluster of job titles you're interested in. You need to be able to name some of those job titles. Second, it defines your Target Market, the group of employers you want to pursue, by specifying their industry, location, and size. You should have a written list of them, a Target List. And third, it contains your central Core Message, aimed at that particular group of Decision Makers, telling them why you are a strong candidate for that particular cluster of job titles.

So the Project Plan insures that you're talking to appropriate Decision Makers in appropriate organizations. And in the most appropriate ways. With a strong Project Plan as the foundation, you are ready to conduct a high quality job search.

Quality and quantity of your search activities

So, to sum it up, regular follow-up with Decision Makers you have contacted is essential to staying out of the dreaded bottom quarter. Having a good Project Plan is also important. So is reading several good job search assistance books, not just this one. All of those are about the quality of your job search.

Your Job Search Work Team can also help you with the quality of your search. That's the purpose of the "advisory panel" discussions that happen in every meeting. With proper attention to the quality of search efforts, very few people need to talk to 124 Decision Makers.

Numerical progress measurements are about the quantity of useful activities. Both quality and quantity are important. But, all in all, it seems to me that the quantity of your effort is the number one factor in job search success, because job hunters often underestimate the required quantity and do far too little. We see that repeatedly in the studies on job search intensity.

The quality of your efforts is very important. But without enough quantity – every week, week after week — the search will probably take too long. You need to make enough contacts and do enough follow-up to get the odds to tip in your favor. That's why you need numerical measurements. And there are some other measures, beyond the two we just discussed.

Other useful progress measurements

I've been talking a lot about informal Decision Maker contacts because most effective job hunters succeed by being proactive: they talk to the Decision Maker before that person admits to having a job opening. But talking to Decision Makers isn't easy. By definition, they're a level above you. You probably don't travel in their social circle. Getting an introduction to them requires some effort.

So suppose you're in a job search and you're not able to find a way to talk to a Decision Maker this week. Your second choice — nearly as good as the first choice — is talking to someone who is more or less at your level inside of an organization you want to work for, a peer contact.

Use Internet research and networking to collect information that allows you to prioritize the employers on your Target List.

Peer Contacts

Why is this useful? Well, those "peer contacts" talk to the Decision Maker regularly. When job hunters get an introduction to a Decision Maker, it's very often through one of those peer contacts. Equally important, that kind of inside contact can provide useful information about job content, organizational culture, the Decision Maker's preferences, and much more. So it's smart to talk to peer contacts before you talk to the Decision Maker.

If you did nothing but talk to peer contacts employed inside of appropriate targeted organizations, that activity alone could produce an invitation to interview. After all, experienced Decision Makers often ask current employees for recommendations when they're thinking about hiring someone. So the number of conversations you have with peer contacts inside of targeted organizations is also an important progress measure.

Very senior executives literally have no peers in organizations where they want to work. So they substitute "influencers" for peers. Those influencers are people who have the ear and the trust of the Decision Makers––who themselves might be board members who are not inside the organization on a day-to-day basis. These influencers might include executives at partners or vendors, as well as consultants and social contacts of the Decision Maker.

Miscellaneous Contacts inside of targeted organizations

If you haven't yet talked to anyone inside of the targeted organization, then talking to any insider at all is useful. At the very least, they can provide a roadmap for you: the names and titles of relevant people, information on how the e-mail system works, information on organizational culture, and more. And they may be able to introduce you to a peer contact or even to a Decision Maker.

So the number of conversations that you have with any "miscellaneous" contacts inside of a targeted organization is also a useful progress measure.

General Network Contacts

The way most job hunters locate all of those "inside contacts" at targeted employers is by talking to people they already know, in other words, general network contacts. This category includes relatives, friends, friends of friends and acquaintances of all kinds.

It usually works like this: you talk to people you know to gather information about potential employers. You use this information to prioritize the list of organizations you want to pursue, your Target List. While gathering information, you also look for people who are comfortable introducing you to contacts at any level inside the organizations on your list.

The job search often moves from conversations with general network contacts to inside contacts and then to the Decision Maker. My informal studies showed that the average job hunter talks to about 11 general network contacts on the way to talking to three inside contacts and one Decision Maker. So talking to enough general network contacts is the first step. And tracking all of these contacts is a central part of measuring your progress. We do this using the Progress Chart on page 73 of this book.

Proactive Job Search

What we're primarily talking about here is Proactive Job Search, the way 50% to 75% of job hunters find jobs. It's about talking to Decision Makers before there is a known job opening. It's usually done by networking. And if you want to be effective about it, you need to be systematic.

You start with a Target List of about 40 potential employers. This is based on the Target Market part of your initial Project Plan, the part that specifies the geographic location, size and industries of the employers you want to work for.

You use Internet research and networking to collect information that allows you to prioritize the employers on your Target List. You always put the most effort into the top of your list, so you're most likely to find a job at the places you like best. And all along the way, you track your progress using the numerical measurements we've been discussing.

Proactive Job Search can also include direct employer contact. This is usually less productive than networking, but it's worth 5% to 10% of your time. It involves contacting Decision Makers to whom you do not yet have an introduction. You use brief, professional written communications and leave repeated, brief, polite voice messages (cold calling). These are all aimed at getting an initial meeting. It's a way of making immediate contact with organizations that are lower on your Target List.

You can find more detailed information on Project Plans, Progress Measurement and Proactive Job Search in my book, *The Unwritten Rules of the Highly Effective Job Search.*

Passive and Reactive Job Search

Of course, you also want to use Passive Job Search and Reactive Job Search. Passive Search is much simpler. You post your resume in the databases of appropriate job boards. You post a LinkedIn profile that aligns with your Project Plan. You contact appropriate recruiters or staffing firms. You do all of this at the beginning of your search, as part of your initial preparation.

Then you wait and see if someone contacts you. If they do, you can very quickly find yourself in a serious formal job interview with a Decision Maker. But while you're waiting, you should definitely be conducting Proactive and Reactive Searches.

Reactive Job Search is the business of reacting to posted job openings. The prize here is the same as in Passive Search: an interview invitation with no networking required. Like Passive Search, Reactive Search is also all about your resume. You find appropriate job postings and you submit your resume, often with a covering e-mail.

Proactive Job Search:

11 general network conversations lead to . . .

3 inside contacts, peer or miscellaneous, which lead to . . .

1 Decision Maker conversation

One interview for every 50 job postings

Progress tracking is important here, too. You need to keep track of how many job postings you have responded to. My rule of thumb here is that you should get one interview for every 50 replies you make to postings. If you have made 75 responses with no interviews, it's probably time to revise your resume, using more carefully selected keywords. Or maybe it's time to revisit your Project Plan and be sure you're going after the right kind of jobs. Your team – or an experienced career professional — can help you figure out what adjustments to make.

Here's another place where the progress tracking is useful: if you are finding only two appropriate postings per week, it's going to take you half a year to get to the 50 that you probably need in order to get one interview. There are many job titles that are rarely advertised, so a lack of postings does not necessarily mean that there are no job openings. It more often means that the employer finds candidates through other channels, including word-of-mouth.

But one thing is clear: You know from your progress tracking numbers that Reactive Search may not be the best route for you. So you put more time into Proactive Search.

On the other hand, maybe you're seeing 20 postings per week. Great! If you're also getting one interview for every 50 responses, Reactive Search is working very well for you and you may not need to do as much networking as most job hunters do.

You may even discover that you get one interview for every 25 responses, routinely beating the rule of thumb of 50. If so, you know that your resume is working very, very well or that there is a very high demand in your field. Or both.

Your progress tracking numbers show you where you stand and how quickly you are moving to-wards that great new job. Your personal goal each week is to see if you can get your numbers a little bit higher than the previous week, and maybe improve the quality of your search a bit as well. The purpose of your Job Search Work Team is to assist you with both of those.

In Chapter Five, The JSWT Manual, you'll see how using progress measurements along with team membership accelerates your progress toward a great new job, and gives you something to be proud of every week. But the progress tracking we've been talking about is only one element of the teams. The manual describes JSWTs in detail and tells you exactly what you need to do in order to start or join one.

But first, in Chapter Four, I want to tell you about the revolution in job hunting and how collaboration, teams and progress measurements are a central part of that. I'll also show you the main elements of a strong job hunting program, so you can decide which ones you want to include in your personal program.

Before you read Chapter Four, take a look at the chart on the next page. It summarizes the progress measurements we talked about in this chapter. And right behind that are some suggestions about how those measurements can be used.

The 10 Categories of Progress Tracking

This chart summarizes the progress tracking that we discussed in Chapter 3. These are the 10 categories used on the Job Search Progress Chart, which is an important tool for job hunters whether they're in a JSWT or not. The categories are defined in more detail on the back of the actual Job Search Progress Chart on page 72.

The numbers in the right hand column are suggested weekly activity levels in each of the categories. These suggestions are for unemployed job hunters. It usually takes some effort and some learning over a period of a month or two in a JSWT to attain these levels.

TOTAL HOURS in job search this week, including all activities	30

JOB POSTINGS – The number you responded to this week	*
DIRECT EMPLOYER CONTACT – The number of initial "cold" contacts	3
DIRECT EMPLOYER CONTACT – The number of follow-up contacts with the above	10

GEN'L NETWORK- Job search conversations with people not employed at targets	22
TARGET MISC.- The number of conversations with insiders not covered below	3
TARGET PEER- The number of conversations with insiders at your level	3
DECISION MAKER (& above)- initial contact only	2
DECISION MAKER (& above)- follow-up contacts with Decision Makers	**

JOB INTERVIEWS # of Decision Maker conversations that were job interviews	***

* This varies widely. Some job hunters find a lot of postings; some find none at all.
** Suggested follow up with Decision Makers is once every three weeks, so this number rises as the total number of Decision Makers you've spoken with rises.
*** Since you cannot control this, there is no suggested number.

Rules of Thumb for Using the Progress Chart Numbers

Here are some of the many ways numerical progress measurements can be used to manage your search project. The top three come from my informal studies. The others are based on estimates made by highly experienced career professionals. You and your team will certainly discover additional ways to use the metrics.

One or two Decision Makers each week

You will not get an offer without first talking to the Decision Maker in your targeted organizations. Once they learn how, most job seekers have conversations with one or two new Decision Makers each week.

Three week intervals on follow-up

Research tells us that follow-up contact with Decision Makers is a key factor in job search productivity – and related to the length of your search. Those with the shortest job searches follow up every two to four weeks with all Decision Makers already contacted every. So as your search gets longer, the number of follow-ups you make each week increases.

14 to 1 ratio

Skilled networkers generally have conversations with 14 other contacts (General Network, Target Misc. or Target Peer) for each Decision Maker they contact. These conversations typically produce introductions to the Decision Makers, as well as the information you'll need to be successful when you talk to them.

50+ direct employer contacts

Making this kind of "cold" contact is worth no more than 5 to 10% of your time each week. The response rate is low, so most job hunters need to make more than 50 initial and follow-up contacts to obtain a single conversation with a Decision Maker. But it's worth doing with organizations where you have do not yet have networking contacts.

20% serious interest

Two out of every 10 Decision Makers you contact should actually conduct a formal job interview with you or say things that indicate you would be a strong candidate if they had an opening. If this does not happen, get more advice on your Project Plan.

50 postings

You should get one invitation to interview for every 50 individual job postings you respond to. If you have responded to more than 50 with no interview, you should check to see if your resume includes the best keywords. And check to be sure you are making the best choices on the postings you're responding to.

CHAPTER FOUR

The Job Search Revolution

In this chapter, I want to talk to you about a professional approach to job hunting. It involves the teams, but it's more than that. It isn't about the skills used or the knowledge needed to find a better job faster. We'll talk about those in Chapter 7, when we discuss how you can put it all together into a good, strong personal job hunting program for yourself.

Right now, I want to tell you about the things career professionals do in the best job search assistance programs. If you have ever used professional assistance in a job search, you may have experienced some of this. But I'll give you an overview of the whole thing. I'll tell you about evolution and revolution in job search assistance programs, so you can get a sense of what's worked – and not worked – over the years.

It's also the story of how and why Job Search Work Teams came to be. And how they fit with other elements of professional job search assistance programs. I'll focus mostly on outplacement services, but programs offered by colleges, nonprofits and government agencies face the same issues, though their evolution has not been exactly the same.

Along the way, I'll tell you more about the teams and how job hunters have reacted to them – and put them to good use. So we'll take a guided tour of the development of job search assistance, including the use of teams. I think this information will help you better understand the methods outlined in the JSWT manual in Chapter 5, and the Chapter 6 tools that it uses.

Here's the story.

The original outplacement service

In 1977, when I got my first job in outplacement, I had never heard of that service. I soon discovered that it was a job search assistance service for people who were let go by larger employers. The service cost thousands of dollars per person, but it was provided as a severance benefit, at no cost to the former employee.

In those days, outplacement services were always provided one-to-one. You were paired with a person called a career counselor. The two of you worked together until you found a new job. The entire service was a one-to-one counseling service.

In the 1970s, most large employers still had an unwritten employment–for–life policy. Once you were hired by one of them, you could reasonably expect to work there until mandatory retirement at age 65. If you lost your job back then, people thought you had been "fired," and must have done something terribly wrong.

In fact, job loss and unemployment were so shameful that people sometimes didn't even tell their families. They left the house in the morning as if they were going to work, but went to the outplacement office instead.

The outplacement counselors worked with their unemployed clients to help them overcome shame, anger and other emotions. That was an important part of the service. After all, you need to be able to speak unemotionally about your last employer in your search for a new job.

After working with a client's emotions, the counselors moved on to helping them evaluate their strengths and weaknesses and using that information to prepare strong communications. The client and counselor also worked together on identifying the best next-step career options, and

Anything that helps job hunters ramp up their performance would help them find better jobs faster.

on resume writing, letter writing, and interview preparation.

The counselor then became a tutor and taught the client networking and other job hunting skills. The client was also given a comprehensive manual, a book covering all aspects of job search, the outplacement firm's entire curriculum. The two then met in weekly one-hour, one-to-one "follow-up" counseling sessions until the client found a new job.

Follow-up sessions were typically unstructured. The counselor helped the client deal with the obstacles, discouragement and disappointment that can accompany job hunting. Those talks often helped job hunters keep their searches moving and helped stalled clients get moving again. The counselor also provided "brush-up" instructions on job hunting methods and helped the client plan the next week's activities.

In outplacement offices, clients were also given private offices or cubicles as well as typing services and free use of a telephone, even for those expensive "long distance" calls.

But the most productive clients––the ones that understood job hunting the best––didn't spend much time in the cubicles. They would stop by the office to talk with their counselor, to make some phone calls or to get some typing done. But between visits, they were not sitting in a cubicle. They were out talking to people.

The cubicle culture

At the other extreme was Charlie, the guy in cubicle #32, who had decorated his workspace with family photos and even put up a little nameplate. Charlie was in the outplacement office every day, from the time it opened until the time it closed. He greeted new clients on their first visit and told them about the difficulties of job hunting and the shortcomings of the outplacement service, as well as how to get their typing done faster and how to get the best cubicle.

Between those two extremes, there were many other job hunters who spent time in the cubicles. Some sought out other job hunters and had useful conversations with them. But some also fell into unproductive "how–bad–it–is" conversations with Charlie.

When someone found a new job, there was no systematic way for others in the cubicles to hear about it –– and learn from that successful job hunter's experience. On the other hand, people often heard about the problems faced by other job hunters. If they didn't hear it directly, Charlie would tell them. But there was no systematic way to hear about the solutions to those problems.

All in all, I think it's fair to say that the "cubicle culture" was not nearly as productive as it could have been. It often failed to support the good work the counselors did. But even more important, there was no organized, systematic way to harness the enormous pool of talent, experience, and know–how moving in and out of the cubicles – and use it to help everyone find great jobs faster.

The more I thought about it, the more it seemed to me that the clients in the cubicles could be organized into work groups where job hunters would actively support each other. They could collaborate to implement what they learned from the counselors. The job hunters were a smart, experienced and diverse group of people. Working together, they could get the job done faster and better than working alone.

But collaboration alone wasn't enough. They also needed a structure, a system to support persistent, productive work — and a productivity-oriented culture to replace the old cubicle culture. For that culture change, we needed to have the most productive job hunters in the work group. And we needed to help Charlie get focused on more effective job hunting.

You need a system to support persistent, productive work.

But how?

I saw the problems and some opportunities, but didn't yet see how to make it all happen.

My search for a breakthrough in job search assistance

As I was making these observations of the cubicle culture in the 1980s, layoffs became more and more common. Outplacement companies grew rapidly and some became global organizations. Large career centers were set up to provide job search assistance, sometimes for mass layoffs involving thousands of people in a single day. The clients, now called "candidates," better understood that job loss was due to no fault of their own.

But the "counseling-plus-follow-up-counseling" program design remained the same, and most job hunters continued to take a less productive, less professional approach to job search. And the unproductive cubicle culture was still the norm.

Job hunters are a smart, experienced and diverse group of people. Working together, they could get the job done faster and better than working alone.

In the late 1980s, I took a course on personal breakthroughs. It was about out-of-the-box thinking, imagining outstanding results and achieving those results by making transformational changes rather than incremental improvements. It seemed to me that some of this could be applied to transforming the cubicle culture into supportive, collaborative work groups.

Work process re-engineering was popular then and I had discussions with other career professionals about re-engineering the outplacement process. And discussions about what a "breakthrough" job search assistance process would look like.

Around that same time, I observed a colleague, Peter Prichard, leading a "peak performance group" with ten job hunters. In a series of eight weekly sessions, he had job hunters set numerical performance goals for their job searches. He posted those on a wall chart. Then he encouraged a great deal of discussion about goals and how to achieve them – making excellent use of the experience in the room.

He taught the group how to use relaxation and visualization techniques, nutrition and exercise as part of improving their performance in job hunting. And he used cognitive psychology and neurolinguistic programming techniques like those discussed by the popular self-help author and motivational speaker, Tony Robbins, in his book, *Unlimited Power*.

After the initial counseling and preparation, it's all about job hunter performance

Peter's approach was an inspiration. He had broken out of the traditional career-counseling paradigm, just as I wanted to do. We agreed that job hunting is a work project where success depends on job hunter performance. So anything that helps job hunters ramp up their performance would help them find better jobs faster.

But I didn't agree with all of the techniques Peter used. And I was interested in an ongoing work team program, not a training. I wanted to have job hunters actually collaborating on getting the work done, assisting each other all the way through it, from beginning to end. And learning by doing.

So seeing Peter's model helped me clarify what I wanted to do in a new breakthrough design:

- Get job hunters out of the cubicles and into a meeting room where they can talk to each other and focus the power of their combined experience, expertise and good judgment on job search success for everyone in the room.

- Replace the cubicle culture with a friendly, supportive, productivity–oriented culture.

- Frame job search — after the initial counseling and preparation — as a team-based work project where performance benchmarks and other project management tools are useful.

- Collect data to determine numerical performance benchmarks useful in job hunting.

- Assist job hunters in increasing the velocity of their job searches by using numerical progress measurements in a supportive and non-judgmental team environment.

I believed that this kind of program could create a revolution in job hunting, one that had job hunters working together in highly productive, peer-group teams rather than toughing it out in solo job searches. It seemed to me that a team-based program would be dramatically more effective than the traditional "follow-up counseling" sessions.

For a work project, you need a work team

The exclusive use of those follow-up counseling sessions didn't make sense to me. At the outset, counseling was useful. But later, when faced with an important work project, you need a team, not a counseling session. Counseling, after all, is about internal work, not managing a work project. With job hunters focused on work, career professionals would need to be team leaders and coaches, not counselors. And many already had those skills.

I also knew that a successful job hunting team would require a clearly defined structure, a process that job hunters and leaders could follow. That was something I had learned the hard way.

Many years earlier, I had attempted to institute a job–club type of program in a large career center. I was working in a job search assistance program that served 2000 unemployed people. I had a staff of outstanding career professionals who did a great job on counseling and teaching, the first part of the process.

For the second part of the process, where people were active in job hunting, I organized job hunters into job clubs that were loosely modeled on Nathan Azrin's Job Clubs.

But I hadn't read Azrin's manual. I didn't write my own manual. And, to tell the truth, I didn't think it through very carefully. The job hunters had been very well prepared, so I thought they would go ahead and collaborate on getting it all done. I thought they'd function as self–directed teams. But that was soon proven to be a naïve assumption.

At the outset, we organized job hunters into clubs and they happily met every week. But we soon started noticing that we had a lot of dropouts. Before long, most of the clubs had a 100% dropout rate within a couple of weeks. Then as the word got around about the clubs, most job hunters simply didn't join them in the first place.

The club program was a notable failure, and one that I could have avoided if I had studied Azrin's manual or thought it through more carefully. It was clear that an effective program wasn't just about putting job hunters into groups and expecting them to collaborate.

That kind of self-directed team requires a great deal of time and effort just to get up to speed. Job hunters need to move much faster, especially if they're unemployed. In hindsight, it was obvious that job hunting groups require a systematic approach.

So in 1991, I designed Job Search Work Teams as a carefully structured program, focused on balancing task and personal support with productivity. I also designed a Job Search Productivity Seminar, with information that would later become the core of my book, *The Unwritten Rules of the Highly Effective Job Search*. That seminar was originally required for all job hunters who wanted to join teams.

I piloted the new JSWT design in a church program in 1991-92. I also introduced it in a small outplacement company where I was working as an outside consultant. And I did the initial research to determine the performance benchmarks and progress measurements we discussed in Chapter 3.

Classroom learning accelerates job hunting

In 1992, Lee Hecht Harrison (LHH), the global career services company, hired me and asked me to institute teams throughout the company. At that time, outplacement was beginning to be called "career transition," and counselors were starting to be called consultants as they added "marketing plans" (also called Project Plans) to the curriculum.

At the same time, LHH was expanding the use of classroom activities for job hunters, so career professionals were doing classroom instruction, using the interaction and discussions that are often part of adult learning.

The two-day LHH workshops offered an opportunity for job hunters to get acquainted with other job hunters – and begin supporting each other and collaborating. So they were a step in the direction of putting the talents of the job hunters to good use.

But equally important, the classroom activities are a better way to teach job hunting than the old one-to-one follow-up sessions. This was particularly evident in the teaching of networking.

Early in my career, I taught hundreds of job hunters how to do networking. I did that in one-to-one counseling and follow-up sessions. But while they nodded in agreement during the session, my clients often didn't actually do very much of what we discussed.

Sometimes they couldn't find ways to do it that they were comfortable with. Other times, they weren't entirely convinced it worked. And some people didn't believe that networking was neces-

A successful job hunting team requires a clearly defined structure. That was something I had learned the hard way.

sary. They thought that want ads and recruiters would do the trick.

But in a workshop, when the leader demonstrated networking in the room, job hunters could see that it produced important information and sometimes even useful introductions – right there in the classroom. So the workshop solved part of the networking problem. But not all of it.

After job hunters left the workshop, they would network energetically for while. But networking rarely produces immediate interviews and job offers. It takes time to gather information and meet the people who can make the right introductions. So, with no immediate results and no progress measurements to show them that they were on the right track, they'd often become discouraged and let up on their efforts.

The job search revolution begins

When I was hired as Corporate Director of Program Design in 1992, LHH decided to move to a more sophisticated program. We retained the initial one-to-one counseling and preparatory work. But we made workshops universally available and then took the revolutionary step of replacing follow-up counseling with Job Search Work Teams led by experienced career professionals.

The JSWTs, of course, go far beyond follow-up counseling or two-day workshops. Team members work together all the way through the project — and actually do the job rather than simply learning it.

New members can see how more experienced members have found a wide range of comfortable ways to network. They see the value of diverse experience and opinions on topics where there is no one "right answer." They see everyone using numerical progress measurements and can connect the numbers with progress toward interviews and offers. And over time, they see other job hunters actually land new jobs using networking.

Why some job hunters hesitated to join teams:

- Fear of numerical measurements

- Negative experiences with other job hunting groups

- Fear of competition

Team members have the same experience with all of the other job hunting methods, too. They see how others use them — and make progress toward results.

So as a way to assist job hunters in managing the work of their job search projects, JSWTs were a revolutionary leap beyond workshops and one-to-one follow-up counseling. But the teams were also a major change, and one that encountered some resistance.

Some job hunters hesitated to join teams

Sometimes job hunters and staff members immediately embraced the new method. They saw that teams could help job hunters more quickly improve their job hunting performance. And have some good company while doing it. Some said things like, "Why didn't we do this sooner? It's so obvious that collaboration makes sense. And everything is done in teams these days."

But sometimes both job hunters and staff members were worried about trying the teams. For some staff members, leading teams was a move away from the one-to-one counseling or classroom instruction that they loved. The addition of team leadership and coaching was an unwanted change in their job description.

Among the job hunters, Charlie, the guy in cubicle #32, was the most threatened. And perhaps with good reason, since the teams focused on productivity in job hunting and he had a lot to learn. He was afraid that the process was too difficult for him and that he'd never be able to get his performance up to a reasonable level.

But it wasn't just Charlie. Other job hunters were also concerned that the numerical measurements would be used to criticize their efforts or publicly embarrass them.

Some job hunters also feared a repeat of previous bad experiences with job hunting groups – so-called "support groups" that were completely unstructured and dominated by sad stories and complaints. Or psychologically oriented groups that helped people feel better, but did nothing to accelerate their progress toward a great new job.

And of course, some job hunters regarded other job hunters as "competition." They feared that talking about their job hunting in a group would result in other people "stealing" the good jobs from them. They thought it was safer to keep their job hunting experiences private.

The fears about progress measurements, complaining, and psychological techniques quickly dissolved once we got a few teams going. Prospective team members talked to experienced members and learned that the teams were safe, comfortable and very useful.

The fears about competition took a little longer. Some job hunters were afraid to talk openly about their job searches, especially if there was someone else in the room looking for jobs with a similar title. This was a serious issue because it tended to undermine the trust needed for successful collaboration.

But those concerns about competition were often overstated. After all, even if two people are looking for exactly the same job title, there are usually significant differences between them. Their expertise or specialties within that job title might be quite different. Their work experience in different companies might be quite different. The organizations they're pursuing might be quite different.

And even if all of that was identical, they're two different people, two different personalities. Some employers will prefer the one; some will prefer the other. It's rarely the head-to-head competition that people think it is.

But fears don't always respond well to logic. So if John was afraid that he was competing with Elizabeth and we had two or more teams operating, we would allow him to join a different team. We also advocated respect for the individual. We never pressed people to divulge information they didn't want to divulge. For example, if they didn't want to say the name of the company where they were interviewing, they weren't urged to do so.

Of course, a job hunter who withholds information can't get the same level of advice and support as one who puts all their cards on the table. So we always looked for ways to increase the trust level so people would be more comfortable sharing information.

Collaboration trumps competition

The most dramatic example I ever saw of overcoming the fear of competition was in a team that I led in New York City. Two team members, I'll call them "Jasmine" and "Karen," were both marketing managers, very similar in age and experience and seeking exactly the same job titles at similar Target Lists of employers. But instead of fearing competition, they flipped the coin over and saw an extraordinary opportunity for collaboration.

They made a pact that whoever landed the first job would continue to assist the other person until she also found a great job. They shared the work of research. They shared information in team meetings and even more between meetings. They coached each other. Over time, they also became friends.

When Karen found a job, she turned over all of her records to her colleague and became an advisor to her. Then Jasmine had the benefit of the team and also of an advisor who was entirely up-to-date on the exact job market she was pursuing. In another six weeks, she also found a job she really liked.

The two of them had never met before they joined the same team. But I suspect that they stayed in touch and became a permanent part of each other's professional networks.

Job Search Work Teams go global

As JSWTs became established in New York, I began to institute the program in other LHH offices. The first time I went to an office outside of the New York area to train staff in the new program, their reaction was, "It's great that those teams worked in New York, but things are different here. JSWT is a New York style program. It will never work here."

But they tried it. And it worked just fine.

The same thing happened again later, the first time I went to London to do a JSWT training. They said, "That's such an American program. It's very different from our ways of doing things."

JSWTs were a revolutionary leap

But again, it worked well – with no changes at all.

The biggest surprise I got involved executive job hunters. I had designed JSWTs for an entry- to mid-level audience of managers and professionals. Executives had the best program money could buy, with access to counselors, consultants and coaches not just weekly but anytime they wanted it. I thought they'd be less interested in teams.

Wow, was I wrong about that! Executives liked the teams better than any other group. And they used exactly the same program design. There was even one case where some executives were driving nearly 100 miles to attend weekly team meetings with other executives. So the use of teams spread through all levels of salaried job hunters at LHH.

By now, the new millennium had begun. Career professionals were commonly called coaches and they routinely did workshops, group process facilitation, coaching, consulting and leadership of JSWTs – as well as career counseling. The Internet made some aspects of job search easier and more convenient. Even though cubicles were still available, the old cubicle culture of individual job hunting faded, replaced by communities of job hunters working with a different value system.

By the early 2000's Job Search Work Teams were well established in LHH. Most LHH offices around the world were successfully using them. Even the Charlie's of the world joined teams. Many teams began using virtual meeting rooms on the Internet to supplement the weekly physical meetings. Later, as LinkedIn became popular, teams set up groups there as well.

JSWT alumni groups

As the use of teams spread, career coaches noticed more and more of the kind of long-term collaboration that Jasmine and Karen had done. They formalized that into JSWT alumni groups. People who met in the teams could then easily stay in touch over the long run. This wasn't just with people with similar job titles. It included everyone on a particular team, a group that was usually similar in compensation level and diverse in job titles.

I was delighted to see the long–term power of the connection formed in the teams. I'd often seen teammates form strong bonds as they worked together, with real friendships sometimes emerging. I hadn't expected those connections to last very long after the job search was completed. But now I know that they sometimes last for years.

I recently talked to a career coach who told me that his team was having its 14th annual reunion. With new members regularly replacing people who find jobs, those JSWT alumni groups can become quite large. And they offer employed people yet another way to create and maintain career–enhancing networks.

Teams in religious communities and nonprofits

The next frontier was the use of JSWTs in nonprofits and religious communities. That started with the publication of my book, *The Unwritten Rules of the Highly Effective Job Search*, which includes a chapter on teams and how to use them. I had always wanted to see the teams available to

everyone, not just those who had access to LHH services. Soon after the book came out, LHH helped me take the first step in that direction.

An LHH manager in Houston invited me to speak at a highly successful church–sponsored job search assistance program. In my talk, I explained progress measurements and JSWTs. Soon after the talk, a group of executive-level job hunters in that program bought the book and began their own teams. Before long, teams were offered to all job hunters in the program.

The same thing happened with two programs sponsored by Jewish Family Services in two different states. And again in a Chicago nonprofit that provided job search assistance for hundreds of job hunters.

These programs sometimes had a dozen teams in operation at the same time, usually with a monthly meeting of all participants that included a job search assistance speaker and a meeting of team leaders. But there were also an increasing number of smaller JSWT programs, usually with just a single team, and often sponsored by a religious community that combined the team meeting with prayer or other religious observance.

The economic problems of 2008 accelerated the growth of all of those programs.

Member-led teams are successful

Most of those programs had no paid staff and no assistance from experienced career professionals. Most of the team leaders were job hunters themselves. So there is now strong evidence that member–led teams can be highly successful. This opens the possibility of faster, more effective, and more comfortable job searches for everyone.

While member-led teams have proven successful, working with a professional career coach is still a big advantage in job hunting. A professional team leader brings expertise in career issues as well as team leadership experience. But not everyone can afford to use one.

So in Chapter 7 we'll take a look at how you can combine teams, coaching and other resources to create a good solid personal job hunting program for yourself that is more effective and more comfortable than solo job hunting. And how you can adjust the amount of professional assistance you use, so you can create a program you can afford — at a price that can be as low as zero.

The heart of the revolution

But now, let's wrap up this chapter by summarizing the job search revolution. I'll start by saying that job search is now more like a team sport than a solo activity. More like volleyball, maybe, than javelin throwing or shot put. So while you might be very serious about winning, you can have some fun with friends while you're doing that.

But it's also a work project, one that you need to organize just like you do with all of your work projects, large or small. And this particular project, since it might not be your favorite activity, needs particular attention to perseverance.

So, with known obstacles to productivity — and a preference for getting it done sooner rather than later – you use performance benchmarks and progress measurements. And you join a team whose central values include collaboration and mutual support.

The revolution, then, is about people working together to get through a sometimes difficult project — and a sometimes difficult life passage. And doing that more comfortably, more effectively and faster than toughing it out alone in a cubicle or a basement office at home.

The American Revolution began with the Declaration of Independence. The job hunting revolution begins with the Declaration of *Inter*-Dependence. Since I found myself writing this chapter

The Heart of the Revolution:

- Job search is a team sport.

- Job search is an organized work project.

- Numerical tracking provides a measure of objectivity.

- Collaboration and support are central values.

just before the Fourth of July, I decided to actually write that second declaration. It's on the next page. It summarizes the beliefs, values and principles that underlie the job hunting revolution and the structure of Job Search Work Teams.

After you take a look at the declaration, the manual in the next chapter will tell you exactly how Job Search Work Teams operate, and exactly what you can do to create one or join one.

The Job Hunter's
Declaration of Inter-Dependence

When in the course of human events it becomes necessary to find a new job, we reject oppressive, outdated, negative ideas. We do not see layoffs, unemployment or job hunting as shameful or embarrassing. We do not see other job hunters as competition. We reject lonely, solo job hunting.

Therefore, we declare that:

• Job search is a team activity where a diverse, experienced and knowledgeable team helps individual members manage their job search projects and land great new jobs faster.

• Career transitions happen more quickly and easily in an interdependent community of people who share their knowledge and experience and work together to improve each other's careers and lives.

• Job hunting is an excellent learning experience, and one where the journey is just as important as the destination.

And we declare our commitment to the following principles:

PRODUCTIVE PARTICIPATION: We fully, actively and enthusiastically participate in improving our own job searches and actively support others in doing the same. We value collaboration.

MUTUAL SUPPORT: We see other job hunters as allies, and we assist them in the work of the search, offer personal support in good times and bad, and always respect their opinions and their individual ways of doing things.

CELEBRATION OF SUCCESS: We celebrate new jobs and career advancement. We celebrate all of the small successes that lead to the large ones. We recognize and honor the effort that leads to these successes.

CHAPTER 5

The Job Search Work Team Manual

If you want to have a successful Job Search Work Team, your top priority is very simple: follow the instructions in this manual.

When I first got the program going at Lee Hecht Harrison, the teams were conducted only by trained and certified professional leaders. These leaders were required to study a 188-page leaders' guide. Their performance as team leaders was evaluated by an observer using a 40–point evaluation form.

Later, when I began working with member–led teams, I discovered that they didn't always follow the instructions. Sometimes they did parts of the program, but omitted elements that are essential to success. And some teams spent a lot of time discussing how to improve the team program, rather than using the time to improve their job searches. As a result, some teams disintegrated before their members found jobs.

But there's no need for that to happen. You can get the great results that we know the teams can produce by reading this 25-page chapter and using it. Once you've read it, you can have the book open in the meeting room while the meeting is going on and do your part even better by keeping an eye on the headings. And after a group of pioneers gets a team going properly, it's easier for the members joining later.

The instructions on the following pages are the result of over 20 years experience and include feedback from dozens of highly experienced career consultants. In refining the program over the years, we tried and rejected many seemingly good ideas that simply didn't work.

If you have suggestions for improving the teams, e-mail them to orville@highlyeffectivejobsearch.com. If it's already been tried and didn't work, I'll tell you why. And if it's an option that has been tried and is known to work in some circumstances, I'll tell you about that. But in the meantime, please follow the instructions in this manual.

We'll start the manual with a more complete description of the teams and what they do. Then we'll cover the guidelines for membership, and what mix of members works best. The manual includes instructions for participating in team meetings and for leading them. Those pages are the part that you might want to use as a reference during the meeting, at least at the outset.

The pages on leading team meetings are important for everyone to read and understand, even if you have a professional leader working with you. We expect to have membership turnover in teams as people find jobs. So if you don't have a professional leader, various team members will serve as team leader — possibly including you. But it's always important for every team member to be familiar with leading teams, because when everyone in the room assists the leader, meetings are more productive.

And finally, there are two ongoing questions about your team: How well is the team functioning? How can you improve its productivity? In the closing pages of this chapter, we'll take a look at how team members and leaders can find answers to these questions. This is important, because after all, the better the team works, the better your personal job search works and the sooner you are likely to find that great new job.

Assist every member in finding a great new job as soon as possible.

Teams do this by improving the quantity and quality of the job search efforts of their members. As you read the following pages of instructions, please notice that everything that happens in the meeting — and all of the recommended activities between meetings — focus on fulfilling this mission.

The Benefits of a Job Search Work Team

JSWTs reduce the amount of time it takes you to find a great new job. Here are some of the ways they do that.

The team serves as:

- **An advisory panel** This enables you to stay objective about your job hunting, focusing on the methods most effective for you. Between team meetings, you also give advice to other members and get advice on topics specific to your personal job search. All of this helps you continuously improve the quality and effectiveness of your search.

- **A personal and task support group** Personal support happens between meetings in pairs or in subgroups, as well as in meetings. Task support is the primary focus of team meetings, and typically involves finding, discussing and understanding the best ways to accomplish specific job search tasks that everyone needs to do.

- **A project management team** Each member is accountable only to themself for their own work, but members use progress measurements to assist each other in managing the search project. This enables you to improve both the quality and quantity of your search activities.

- **An effective core network** Based on team members' solid knowledge of each other's plans and targets, they can help each other with information gathering and sometimes even with introductions. The longer you're in a team, the better other members get to know you, your Project Plan and your approach to job hunting. The better they know all of that, the better they can assist you in the meeting and between meetings.

As a team member, you are more likely to:

- **Stay focused and on the right track** Public reporting of numerical progress measurements is a key to this kind of focus. Observing what works––and what does not work––for others is an enormous timesaver because it accelerates your learning curve. The Final Report to the Team (see page 91) is also a central part of this learning.

- **Maintain a reasonable level of job search intensity** As we discussed earlier, the research clearly shows the importance of job search intensity. Numerical progress reporting is how JSWTs support that intensity. Each member tries each week to improve upon their previous average numbers. The team supports that effort and celebrates individual successes.

- **Keep your search moving** In Final Reports to the Team, members often say something like, "I wanted to look my best at the team meeting, so I put in some extra effort even though I had a difficult week." Members use the weekly meetings as a motivator. This is the "accountability" part of the process. Job hunters are accountable only to themselves, but they formalize that by reporting to the team.

- **Become more effective in job hunting** A central purpose of JSWTs is quantitative and qualitative improvement of job search effectiveness. The better you are at job hunting, the sooner you will successfully complete your job search. This is the best available guarantee of success in job hunting.

Membership in a Job Search Work Team

- **A team has 6 to 12 members** Members are replaced as they land jobs. Having more members means you have more knowledge, experience and resources in the room for each meeting. But with over 12 members, the meeting becomes difficult to manage.

- **Active in search** Members must be actively looking for a job. This means that each member must have some numbers higher than zero on the Progress Chart every week. They need to have completed enough of their preparation that they are ready to begin talking to people and conducting an active search.

- **Employed/Unemployed** Job hunters who are employed in full-time jobs must be on separate teams from unemployed job hunters. This is because the two groups work at very different rates of speed. Employed people need only two team meetings per month, but unemployed people should meet weekly.

  Employed job hunters should also be looking for new possibilities inside of their current employers, and, of course, it's important that they pay attention to keeping their current job until they find a new one. So the advisory panel discussions are different in teams for employed people. There are more suggestions for these teams on page 58.

- **Employed part-time** Job hunters who are employed part-time can join teams of unemployed people. They must always be available at the appointed meeting time and their work schedule must allow enough time for a full-blown job search. This usually means working three days a week or less.

- **Diversity** A diverse membership is a plus, but homogeneous groups also work. Senior executives often prefer their own separate teams, but subgroups of executives have been successfully included in teams of mid-level managers and professionals. A wide range of functions, job titles and industries is an advantage, since each brings different skills and perspectives.

- **Consulting/project work** Team members who accept consulting assignments or project work are put "on hold" until they complete the assignment. When "on hold," they do not attend meetings or use a Progress Chart. They retain their membership and return at the end of the assignment.

Adding New Members

Job Search Work Teams quickly learn the importance of recruiting new members to replace those who find jobs. Teams that fail to do this can shrink to a size where they don't operate as well. A team of 6 to 12 members provides a rich array of knowledge and resources, while keeping the meetings manageable. A smaller team has fewer resources.

Sources of new JSWT members:

- **Networking groups** for job hunters can be one-time events or ongoing programs. They are great places to meet other job hunters who might want to join your team. Online groups are also possible, though of course, you'd want to get acquainted in person before inviting someone to join.

- **State employment services** sometimes offer training sessions or other group meetings. Team members who participate in these can invite people they meet to join their team.

- **Job search programs sponsored by religious communities,** as well as those sponsored by nonprofits, including libraries, are also great sources of new team members. In the absence of such programs, religious professionals often know which members of their congregations are unemployed. And they may be willing to make announcements about your team.

Any of these groups can be an ongoing source of job hunters from which individual teams can recruit new members. Some of them may want to sponsor teams, or integrate them into existing programs, if you explain what you're doing and show them this book.

Getting Started with New Members

As you bring new members into your team, it's important to get them up to speed quickly. Their fresh insights will be an asset. But you don't want them to slow the team's progress by spending too much time in their initial meetings on job hunting basics. Or inadvertently disrupting the meeting's normal process. So have new members:

- **Visit the team** for one meeting without participating before they join. This gives them the opportunity to see how things work.

- **Work with an experienced team member** outside of team meetings for two or three weeks. That experienced "coach" assists the new member in becoming a highly productive team member as quickly as possible.

The Team Meeting

Meetings are held at the same time and place each week and last a maximum of two hours. Because this is a work meeting and not a social event, it's very important that all meetings start exactly on time and conclude in two hours or less. Serious job hunters have work to do and may have appointments scheduled. Informal discussions and socializing are encouraged, but outside of the meeting, not during it.

Each meeting includes:

1. Pre-meeting preparation of Weekly Reports
Team members prepare their Progress Reports (below) before arriving, since discussions with other members before and after the meeting are valuable and it's important to start the meeting on time. Weekly Report tent cards (page 77) are used to display progress-reporting numbers at every meeting. These can be completed before arriving or in the room just before the meeting.

2. Progress reporting
(3 minutes per person) Each team member provides a verbal report on their progress in job search during the previous seven days. The person reporting may also propose an agenda item for discussion, if they have one. Three minutes per person is the maximum time for these reports. Please see page 46 for the content of the report.

This reporting is important because it fosters accountability for the search and helps individuals maintain reasonable search intensity. It also helps team members understand each other's searches, which is a learning opportunity and also the basis for providing each other with advice and assistance.

But while reporting is essential, the most important part of the meeting is the advisory panel. So you need to keep the total reporting time to 36 minutes or less to allow plenty of time for discussion. And remember, never mix discussion with the reporting.

3. Agenda creation
(4 minutes) Creating the agenda is one of the team leader's most useful tasks in the meeting. It customizes each meeting to the needs of the people in the room. It determines the value members will get from the longest part of the meeting.

The team works best when every member understands how to create the agenda and prioritize it, so the most important issues get the most time. Then the leader doesn't have to work so hard and the meeting moves along better.

All members should understand what issues are appropriate for team discussion and what issues should be discussed in a sub-group outside of the meeting. Everyone should know how to formulate an agenda item as a question that will produce information useful to everyone in the room, as well as the person who asked it. Agenda items should be "actionable," practical suggestions that can be put to use immediately. You'll see more about this on page 47.

4. Advisory panel discussion of agenda items
(approximately 85 minutes). Once the agenda has been created and prioritized – with time limits for each item — it's not difficult for the leader to facilitate a discussion of the agenda items.

It's not the leader's job to provide answers to the questions on the agenda. That's the job of the entire team, which is why it's so important for members to attend all meetings and to read some job hunting books.

The more members who participate in discussing agenda-item questions, the better. A good discussion provides a number of different viewpoints on each question — which is useful since there's not usually a one-size-fits-all answer.

Because it's important to hear from a number of different people, it's important that no one person takes too much time. If ten members are in the room for a 80-minute discussion, then each person's fair share of time would be 8 minutes.

But since some people naturally speak more often or give longer answers than others, I like to use 15 minutes per person as a rule of thumb for total maximum airtime in the discussion. Of course, if there are only six team members in the room, that number would be increased accordingly. There is rarely a need to monitor this.

While the fair and reasonable use of "air time" is important, the central rule in conducting discussions is not to "pile on" the person who asked the question. For example, if a team member named Orville asked the question, "How can I get more useful referrals in a networking meeting with a friend," team members should remember that both the question and the responses to it should benefit everyone, not just Orville. And that not all of the suggestions will work well for Orville.

So no one should ever be shaking their finger at Orville and telling him that he's got to do less of this and more of that. Or that he was mistaken in his approach. Or that he needs to work harder.

Understanding that the questions and the answers are for everyone, team members should simply toss out ideas and suggestions, based on their experience and their reading. Orville should listen for the ones that might work for him. And everyone else should listen for advice useful to them. Suggestions are for everyone.

5. Meeting wrap-up (0 to 4 minutes) This optional section of the meeting might include election of a new alternate team leader or other "housekeeping" items. It is also the time when a new member signs the JSWT Contract (see page 67).

6. Optional post-meeting discussions After the meeting ends, some members may want to stay in the meeting room to have one-to-one or small group discussions.

How to Give a Progress Report

Each week, each team member gives a three-minute progress report including these items:

1. Your numbers Read the current week's numbers from your Progress Chart so others can better understand how you're managing your job search. Everyone knows what the numbers mean, so it's best if you simply read the pairs of numbers – last month's average and this week's number — without comment. Hold up your Weekly Report tent card so members can see the numbers in writing. This can be done in 30 seconds.

2. Three highlights. These are the three best things that you did or that happened to you in job hunting in the last seven days. They could include: a major breakthrough; a small step in the right direction; a problem solved; or a "gift from God," something useful that came your way with no effort on your part.

Everyone must name three highlights every week. This is important because sometimes job hunters don't give themselves credit for the step–by–step progress that they are making. It's also useful to other team members, who may notice that they can replicate some of the good things on your list.

In preparing this part of your report, think back over the last seven days. Make a mental (or written) list of everything you did and everything that happened to you in your job search. Prioritize that list, with the most useful things at the top and the least useful at the bottom. The three items at the top of your list are your three highlights.

Think of each of these highlights as a story, long or short. Give each story a descriptive title. Then, in your report, mention the three titles with just a little elaboration on each. If you tell all three stories from beginning to end, your report will exceed three minutes. If some members want to hear the entire the story, you can tell them after the meeting.

3. Three priorities Tell the team your three top job search priorities for the coming week. Like your highlights, your priorities are something you should think about before you arrive at the team meeting. Each week, review your Project Plan and your Target List. Zoom out from your day-to-day activities to see where you are. Then ask yourself what are the most important things you need to do in the coming week.

This should always include pursuit of several targeted organizations where you have so far made little or no progress. Mentioning those organizations by name as part of your priorities report has the added advantage that it reminds other team members what organizations are on your Target List. If they have useful information, they can say, "I've got something for you on that one. Talk to me after the meeting."

But never divert from the report into a discussion of the target companies. This would leave the rest of the team sitting and waiting while someone provided information that would probably be useful only to you. So do that after the meeting.

4. Your agenda item (optional) Here is your opportunity to tell the team--your advisory panel--what you would like to discuss and get their assistance with. If there was something that did not go well in your job search in the last seven days, that might be a good agenda item. Or if you are not sure how to approach something that you have planned for the next week, that's another good possibility. Even if you had an outstanding week, there might still be an area that you want to improve on.

Agenda items should always be about job search itself, not preparation for search (e.g., resume writing). And they should always be immediate and practical job search issues. You want to get advice and suggestions that you can use in the next seven days. Vague and theoretical agenda items – like "I want to discuss networking" — are of little use to you or anyone else. On the other hand, a specific networking question like, "What are the best ways to follow up with a friend who introduced me to someone inside a target company," will probably provide information that's useful to you and everyone else.

In that last example, please notice how it was generalized. It's not about your friend Susan and how she introduced you to someone at Amalgamated Services. It's about an introduction from a personal contact to an insider at a target, something that applies to everyone. And it's phrased as a question so everyone will know what you need.

Job search issues that do not apply to anyone but you should be handled outside of the meeting, not as agenda items. If you need advice on that kind of question and aren't sure which team member to ask, raise the question in this section of your report and ask the leader to help you find a team member to assist.

Members are not required to have an agenda item every week. But if you rarely have one, it's probably because you're not thinking carefully enough about your job search.

Examples of focused and generalized agenda items:

- *What's the best way to follow up with a Decision Maker after an informal meeting?*
- *How can I get more information in discussions with personal contacts about my Target List?*
- *How do I decide which executive recruiters to contact?*

Issues like these should be discussed outside of the team meeting:

- *I might want to do some consulting, but I'm not sure what kind of consulting to do.*
- *I need to expand my Professional Objective to include more potential job titles and I need some suggestions on what titles are best for me.*
- *My spouse thinks I'm not working hard enough on my job search and we're getting into arguments about it. I need some advice.*

The JSWT Contract:
An Essential Element of Team Success

If you want your team to provide the advantages we discussed in Chapters 2, 3 and 4, you must require all members to sign the JSWT Contract. Without the contract, a JSWT soon becomes a loosely organized drop–in discussion group that's not likely to accelerate anyone's job search and not likely to retain serious job hunters as members.

The JSWT Contract creates a committed work group made up of people who are serious about success in job hunting and aligned with the mission of getting all team members into good new jobs ASAP. Using the contract intensifies personal and task support among members and increases the job search intensity that research shows is essential to success.

The following are the six agreements that make up the JSWT Contract, with an explanation of the importance of each. Before participating in a team, all members are required to sign the shorter version of the contract on page 67.

All members must sign the JSWT Contract, agreeing to:

1. Attend/report All members agree to use the JSWT Progress Chart (see page 73) and provide progress reports every week without exception, whether they attend the meeting or not. Members also commit to attending every meeting unless they have a personal emergency, an illness, an important family event or a job interview that cannot be scheduled at any other time. Absent team members transmit their report to another member who reads it to the team. Reports from absent members do not include agenda items, since the person will not be present for the discussion.

As we discussed, the team functions as an advisory panel to individual members. Each team member is a resource to other members. If you are not at the meeting, that's one less resource that team members can use for information, advice, and networking. So your presence at the meetings is important to the team.

There are two more reasons why this agreement is important. First, there is a tendency for people to think about skipping the report – and the meeting — when they had a difficult week in job search. But if you have had a week when things didn't go well in your search, that's the week you most need to attend the team meeting. Otherwise, your productivity is likely to slip. Second, the team needs to be up-to-date on what's going on with your search so they can be useful to you.

2. Two to four hours Members agree to volunteer two to four hours each week to assist one or more team members between meetings. This does not mean that you will necessarily use those hours every week. Nor does it mean that you are required to do anything that anyone asks of you.

The spirit of this commitment is that you actively look for ways that you can assist other team members each week. If you are honestly unable to find a way to do that every single week, that's okay. The agreement is simply that you will try.

It is also important that you do not exceed the four hours. Your primary responsibility is your own job search.

3. Respect other team members
The most important examples of this are: Take only your fair share of meeting time. Never attack or belittle anyone about anything. Arrive early for meetings, not merely on time. Resign in person at a regular meeting if leaving the team without a new job.

4. Donuts and debriefing
When you land a job, debrief the team and buy them refreshments. The debriefing is based on the Final Report to the Team on page 91. You can do it in person, or transmit a report in writing. Sharing information on what made you successful helps others be successful.

You can provide something better than donuts if you prefer. The food is for the team's celebration of your success. Members agree to have both of these items delivered by another team member if they have started a new job and cannot attend.

5. Three books
Read at least three job hunting books in the first 90 days of team membership, one or more per month. This is important for all teams, and absolutely essential for those without a professional leader. Knowledge of job search methods is essential and all team members need to contribute to that. Otherwise, it can become a case of the blind leading the blind.

You can find recommended books at www.highlyeffectivejobsearch.com. *The Unwritten Rules of the Highly Effective Job Search* is strongly recommended for everyone, because that book explains Project Plans and the other methods that are the basis for these teams. Beyond that, it's useful for different members to read different books to bring a wide range of knowledge into the room.

6. Follow the guidelines
Like any team, this one functions best when everyone is following the same set of rules, so it's important to follow the guidelines in this book. Job Search Work Teams are emphatically not self-directed teams. They employ a structured process proven to work in job hunting. Self-directed teams, those that invent their own rules, require a great deal of time to create an appropriate work process. The JSWT process is already created, fully tested and known to produce results.

These six agreements form the contract that makes the team effective. Job hunters who are not willing to make these agreements should not join a team. If someone makes the agreements and joins a team, but later repeatedly fails to keep the agreements, they must be asked to leave the team. More on this on page 55.

Team Leadership

In a Job Search Work Team, everyone leads.

When everyone knows how to do their part in the meeting, the leader doesn't have to work so hard, and the team is more beneficial to everyone. So all members need to understand team leadership. This is true even if the team has a career professional as a leader.

Member-led teams always have people designated as Leader and Alternate Leader as well as Timekeeper and Alternate Timekeeper. The alternates are important in case the Leader or Timekeeper have to miss a meeting – and because we hope and expect that they will soon find a job and need to be replaced with little notice.

Leaders are elected by secret ballot for a three-month term. They can be re-elected. They can resign from leadership without leaving the team. They should be chosen based on knowledge of job hunting and ability to lead group discussions without taking more than their share of airtime. A new team elects a leader and an alternate. Then, any time a leader or alternate finds a job and leaves, a new alternate is elected immediately.

The secret ballot avoids offending anyone, and the three-month term prevents any one person from being overly burdened by the role. Timekeepers are appointed by the leader.

Leadership matters most in these seven areas:

1. Reporting

The leader starts the meeting exactly at the appointed time. This is an important part of maintaining the team meeting as a work meeting, rather than an informal social event. If any member is absent, the leader asks who will give that person's report.

If the absent member has not transmitted a report to anyone, the leader selects a volunteer to telephone the absent member immediately after the meeting, check to make sure they're okay, and remind them of their agreement to send in reports when they're absent. The leader makes a note to request a double (two-week) report from the person at the next meeting.

Reporting proceeds clockwise around the table, with the leader reporting last, in the same way that other members report. The timekeeper quietly times each report, giving a hand signal at two minutes and 45 seconds, and politely interrupting the person at three minutes if the report isn't concluded by then.

2. Agenda creation and prioritization

The leader ensures that everyone's job search advice and assistance needs are met, either in the advisory panel discussion or in a meeting with an individual or subgroup after the team meeting.

As members give their reports, the leader may sometimes need to provide reminders of what to include, for example: "Please don't forget your third highlight."

Sort and record the items. When a member mentions an agenda item that is not appropriate for discussion in the meeting (see page 47), the leader asks for one or more volunteers to assist that person with it at some time after the meeting. When the agenda item is appropriate for discussion, the leader makes sure it is phrased as a question that accurately reflects the member's need.

The leader then records it on a flipchart or whiteboard, with the member's initials next to the question. If no flipchart or whiteboard is available, the leader repeats the question, and the leader — and each team member — records it on paper so they can refer to the list of questions as the meeting proceeds.

Vote to prioritize the items. When all members have given reports, the leader prioritizes the agenda items by asking members to vote for the three items they are most interested in discussing. The time-keeper counts the votes and the number of votes is recorded next to each item. The leader then prioritizes the items, numbering them according to how many votes they received, from most to least.

Assign time allocation to items. The leader then assigns a time allocation to each agenda item, with more time for those that received more votes or might require more time. The total of the time allocations should be about ten minutes less than the time remaining in the meeting. If there is no flipchart, all members should record these time allocations.

Once this procedure is learned by the leader and the team members, it very quickly sets up an advisory panel discussion that is likely to be productive and useful for all members.

If there are too many items to discuss in the meeting, the leader looks to see if any two can be combined into a single item before the vote. Or the leader asks for volunteers to handle some lower-priority items in a sub-group after the meeting. Carrying agenda items over to the next meeting does not work well, because the best items have real time value — they're things someone is working on right now. And the next meeting will have its own list of items.

If there are too few items, the leader asks the team for more before prioritizing them. One agenda item for every two people in attendance is a useful rule of thumb.

3. The advisory panel discussion

The leader refers the team to the first agenda item and asks the member who raised it to repeat the question and elaborate a little. Members then volunteer a range of ideas and suggestions that could answer the question. These are not critiqued or evaluated by the team. They are simply shared with everyone.

Team Leadership (continued)

About halfway through the allotted time, the leader asks the person who raised the question if the discussion is going in a direction that is useful to them. If necessary, the person refines the question or re-directs the conversation.

Before the end of the allotted time, the leader asks the person who raised the question if they got some suggestions that they can use. If so, this discussion can be wrapped up a bit early. In concluding the discussion, the leader may summarize some of the key points. The leader can add their own suggestions to the summary, if they weren't mentioned earlier.

If the time limit is reached before an item's owner has heard some suggestions they can use, the leader asks for volunteers to discuss it further with the person after the meeting.

The leader then moves to the next agenda item. As the discussion continues, it's important for the leader to complete each item in the allotted time or less. If all agenda items are covered in less than two hours, the leader adjourns the meeting early. This is a business meeting and members may have appointments following it, so concluding on time or early is part of respecting fellow team members.

Creating cultural norms. High-functioning teams are particularly effective because they have well-established cultural norms. A strong leader creates these norms not by talking about standards or enforcing rules, but by modeling and facilitating desired behaviors. Walking the talk, in other words, and empowering others to walk the talk.

An important example of this is the use of the Two to Four Hour agreement. Rather than just urging members to use those hours as agreed, a strong leader might say things like:

> *Fred, would you like some assistance with the use of that job board? ("Yes.") George, you seem particularly knowledgeable in that area. Would you be willing to assist Fred with it this week?*

> *Susan, Jason, Jose and Amanda, all of you have mentioned concerns about interviewing. Would you be interested in a practice session? (Four "yesses.") Susan, would you be willing to lead that group? Anyone else want to join?*

As team members complete between-meeting activities, a strong leader checks in with them in informal chats — before the meeting — to see how things went. The leader might mention the most successful activities, in the meeting wrap-up or in a discussion, to reinforce and publicize the success. Team members should routinely assist with this by mentioning successful between-meeting activities in the highlights section of their reports.

In time, this kind of behavior creates a culture where between-meeting assistance happens regularly and without any leader facilitation. Then new members joining the team tend to pick up on the behavior, since it's obviously "the way we do things around here."

4. The meeting wrap-up

This could be a brief as, "Thank you. See you next week." Or it could include any of the following:
- A new member contract signing and welcome
- Election of a new alternate leader
- Routine, brief "housekeeping" items

5. Final Reports to the Team: 15 minutes or less

When a team member lands a new job, a celebration is certainly in order. But the celebration must not interfere with the normal functioning of the team, since there are other members who have not yet landed jobs. So here's the recommended way to handle that happy event.

When someone has landed a job, there are donuts or some other refreshments on the table. If the "lander" is able to attend, there is usually some real excitement. Everyone wants to hear the news.

So the very first event in the meeting, before the progress reports begin, is the lander's Final Report to the Team. If the lander is there in person, they give the report, following the instructions on page 91 and using notes they have prepared or reading their written report. After the report, the lander answers any questions members may have.

If the lander is not present, then the team leader locates the person who has their Final Report, and that person reads it to the team. If the lander is present, but has not prepared a Final Report, the leader guides them through a verbal report by asking the questions in the Final Report to the Team. If the lander does not have a record of the requested progress numbers, the leader asks them to estimate those numbers.

Following the Final Report, there is a tendency for members to want to celebrate immediately. However, it's important for those who have not yet landed to get back to work on job hunting and not substitute a celebration for a team meeting.

So the entire Final Report must be completed in 15 minutes or less. Since they now have a job, the lander is no longer a team member. They're now an alum. They are welcome to stay for the team meeting as a visitor, but of course, they have no progress report.

Most teams continue the celebration of the landing immediately after the team meeting, in the meeting room or at a nearby restaurant or coffee shop.

6. Selecting new members

The team leader may select new members or delegate that job to one to three members. One person should meet the prospective member. Others may also take a look at the person's resume. The most important factor is that the person is in the team's general compensation range. Some teams also check for head-to-head competition with other members, and if it seems to exist, they have the two talk to each other.

It's important to decide to accept the person before they visit the team. Job hunters have enough rejection and shouldn't be subjected to a visit and a strenuous JSWT selection process that might end in yet another rejection. Once someone is invited to visit a team meeting, they should be automatically accepted if they want to sign the contract and join.

Involving the entire team in making a decision to accept a new member is unnecessarily complex. And voting — even by secret ballot — leaves a new member forever wondering who voted against them. The best policy is keeping it simple and informal. If someone later insists on behaving badly, you can ask them to leave.

7. Unproductive team behavior

I'm happy to say that in the many years I've worked with Job Search Work Teams, unproductive behavior on the part of team members has been rare. But it does sometimes happen, and when it does, it's important to correct it immediately – before it interferes with the team's mission. Here are the problems that sometimes arise and suggestions for handling them.

The Attend/Report Agreement. The most common problem is that a member fails to send in a report when they're absent. We already mentioned the remedy for this, in "Reporting," on page 50. The leader asks someone to phone the person, and the person is expected to give a report for two weeks at the next meeting and display two Weekly Report tent cards (like the one on page 77), one for each of the two weeks.

It's important for the leader to follow up on the two-week report if the person who was absent doesn't volunteer it. If the person hasn't prepared a report for the missed week, the leader should ask them to do it on the spot, as well as they can remember it. Numbers and Highlights are sufficient for the missed week, since Priorities and Agenda Items are no longer relevant.

Why go to this trouble? Because if missed reports are tolerated, the team's unspoken cultural norm is that the "Attend/Report" agreement really doesn't matter. Then no one takes it seriously. It's a short step from there to the conclusion that the entire contract is not taken seriously. And without the contract, the group is no longer a Job Search Work Team. It becomes an informal discussion group that may have no connection to shorter and more effective job searches.

The most effective teams are effective because they have established cultural norms that support productivity, effectiveness in task and genuine personal support of all members. Honoring the Attend/Report agreement is usually the first step in that direction.

The Respect Agreement. The JSWT should be a place where job hunters feel supported in their efforts to succeed in the sometimes unpleasant business of job search. So it's important that no one be publicly criticized or attacked.

Sometimes a team member who wishes to assist another team member does so by publicly critiquing them. If someone else publicly criticizes the critiquer, then the second person is also engaging in the unwanted behavior.

The solution, of course, is to speak with the person privately, gently and politely about how their comments, though intended to help, might actually be received as unsupportive or even belittling. The leader should do this, and other team members can as well.

Other negative talk — complaining about job hunting or the "job market," for example — that sometimes occurs in a team meeting is more easily handled. If the complaint is about job hunting, the leader should invite the job hunter to convert the complaint into an agenda item, and figure out what they're going to do about it in their own search. If the complaint is about something that no team member can control, then it has no place in the meeting because it doesn't support the team's mission.

Asking a member to leave the team. We all know that job hunting can be stressful, and that stressed people sometimes don't behave as well as they'd like to. So, of course, you want to give everyone every chance to behave productively. However, the six agreements — particularly "attend/report" and "respect" — are essential to the team's functioning and must be taken seriously.

If a team member repeatedly indulges in negative behavior – behavior that is clearly and unequivocally in violation of the contract they signed – they must be asked to leave the team. Even though you would prefer to retain the member and assist them, the choice will ultimately be between losing that member or doing permanent damage to the entire team.

Here's the standard penultimate speech — delivered in private, of course — for someone with repeated violations:

> *Bob, I want to be clear that it's not necessary for you to be on a Job Search Work Team. Thousands of people find jobs without joining a team. If the team is not working for you, then you should find another way to complete your job search. But if the team is working for you and you want to stay with it, then you must observe all of the commitments you made in the contract you signed. Which would you prefer?*

If Bob has read this book and has been spoken to about his behavior before, then he shouldn't be surprised by the speech. And if he hasn't read the book and seen the little speech above, well then that's yet another reason why maybe he shouldn't be on a Job Search Work Team right now.

Before asking someone to leave the team, the leader should privately speak to a majority of the other members to be certain they agree with that decision. Then the person is privately notified of the decision. Once again, this kind of thing is rare. But if it happens, it must be handled.

Mistakes to Avoid

These are the most common mistakes. If not corrected, all of them slow the team's progress, and some can actually cause the disintegration of the team. If one of them happens in your team, don't discuss it during the team meeting. Discuss it with the leader after the meeting. Please notice that all of these violate the "follow the guidelines" agreement.

- **Changing or neglecting the progress reporting.** Some teams are highly enthusiastic about reporting and want to report on 20 or 30 items instead of just a few. But extensive reporting is simply not worth the time it takes in the meeting.

  Another mistaken direction is tracking items that don't directly relate to progress, such as attendance at job fairs. Progress is about the number and type of conversations you had, not the event at which you had them.

  At the other extreme, some teams decide they want to curtail or eliminate progress reporting. The group then stops being a JSWT. It doesn't support the job search intensity needed for success.

- **Mixing discussion into progress reporting.** Sometimes a team member raises a good agenda item and the team immediately dives into discussing it. Or a team member has an intriguing "highlight" that invites immediate discussion.

  If this is permitted, it leads to a disorganized meeting that does not make the best use of time, because the selection of topics is not focused on the needs of the whole team. It also makes progress reporting too long. Then there's insufficient time for agenda items that may be more important than the ones spontaneously discussed.

- **Using "goals" instead of "priorities."** Enthusiastic about the use of numerical progress reporting, some teams want members to publicly state numerical goals for the coming week, as in, "I talked to one Decision Maker this week. My goal for next week is two Decision Makers."

  The problem with this approach is that when members publicly announce goals and then fail to achieve them, they're publicly embarrassed and might spend time making excuses for the "failure."

  It's a negative event for everyone and poor use of time. So it's better to let those who like to set personal numerical goals do that privately rather than publicly.

- **Weekly leader rotation,** rather than a single leader who stays with it. This usually results in less consistent and weaker leadership. Instead, select the best person, and then let them get even better through experience.

- **Frequent change of meeting time or place** usually results in people missing meetings and requires too much date/time communication.

How You Know It's Working:
Signs that Your Team Is on the Right Track

The following are all good signs, indicators that the team is working well. It usually takes a new team a few weeks to get up to speed on these. And some, like retention and job placements, can only be judged over a longer time.

- **Progress reporting is well established.** Progress reporting begins exactly on time every week, whether the leader is present or not. Members give good reports, following the format without prompting. The reports generally take a little less than three minutes per person, with no assistance from the timekeeper.

- **The advisory panel discussion is effective and popular.** People are clearly interested, engaged and generally happy during the discussion. Most members participate in the discussion most of the time, but no one – not even a professional leader — dominates the conversation. If you ask them, members will pretty much always say that they learned something about more effective job search.

- **Final Reports to the Team are always used,** every time someone lands a job.

- **Everyone is happy with the team's leadership,** and says so, publicly and privately.

- **100% of members always honor the contract agreements.** This is usually because all members have carefully read this book and visited the team before they signed the contract and joined the team — and because those agreements are firmly established as cultural norms.

- **100% retention.** Members never leave the team unless they have a new job they're happy with. Or unless an event in their personal life requires it.

- **The team's culture is generally friendly, supportive, task-oriented and effectiveness-oriented.**

- **Your team has a name.** A subgroup comes up with several possibilities outside of the meeting. The team votes to select one of them as a "housekeeping" item.

If one of these is not working as well as you'd like it to, do not discuss it during the meeting. Doing that takes the team backwards by spending meeting time on something that doesn't directly support the mission. Instead, discuss it outside of the team meeting, as a whole group or as a subgroup of volunteers.

The solution to most problems can be found in this book, so the first step should always be re-reading the appropriate chapters. And it's a good idea to re-read this chapter at least once in the initial weeks of your team membership, to make sure you're doing your part to make it work for everyone – including you.

Virtual Teams

Virtual teams are more difficult, especially without an experienced professional leader. But online and telephone meetings are possible. Here are some suggestions:

- Limit the membership to a group of four to seven.

- Reduce the total meeting time to a maximum of 90 minutes.

- Instead of Weekly Report tent cards, the team uses an Internet site where all members post their numbers at the end of the day prior to the meeting. All members then refer to the progress numbers on that site during progress reporting.

- It's essential that all members record all agenda items as they are formulated, so that everyone can see them. Or the team can use an Internet site that allows the leader to post the items for all to see as the meeting progresses.

- The leader should be sure that members are invited to participate in discussions, so that there is broad participation in agenda item discussions.

- Be sure to have one-to-one phone conversations between members between meetings, perhaps by requiring every member to talk to two others each week. E-mail blasts and other leader communications are also useful.

- This kind of team works better if it holds at least one in-person meeting before beginning virtual meetings.

Teams for Job Hunters with Full-Time Jobs

Job hunting while employed full-time is more complex. Job hunters have much less time and energy to devote to a job search, so their Progress Charts will probably show about one-quarter the activity of unemployed job hunters. They also need to be cautious about their job hunting, since employees known to be looking for new jobs are sometimes seen to be less interested – and can therefore be more likely to be included in a layoff. And it's usually a good practice to be looking for new possibilities within the current employer, as well as outside.

Here are some suggestions for this kind of team:
- Limit membership to four to seven. Do not include people who are unemployed.
- Have a two-hour, in-person meeting twice a month, on a regular meeting day – first and third Wednesday evenings, for example. Have confidentiality agreements.
- Set up subgroups that members can use to discuss their personal current work situations with other members between team meetings – to look for ways to improve the situation or to move to another job within the organization.

Team-Based Programs for Students

There are two options for a team-based job search assistance program for students. I'll provide a quick conceptual sketch of each. In the real world, of course, an effective program is more complex than these sketches.

Option #1: On-campus JSWTs continue after graduation or merge with alumni teams.

With this model, college career services focus on preparation for job search in the first half of the students' last year on campus. This includes a Project Plan (Professional Objective, Target Market and Core Message), a Target List, a resume, a LinkedIn posting and the like. This can be done in "preparation teams," or in one-to-one sessions.

In the second half of the year, students join a JSWT that meets once or twice a month, with meetings timed to dovetail with the school's calendar. Job search activity levels are expected to be similar to teams for employed people. To the degree possible, membership is according to the planned city of destination after graduation. So students planning to live in New York City are in one team, those heading for Los Angeles in another team.

If in-person teams in destination cities are impractical for some students, they can set up virtual teams before leaving the campus.

The on-campus teams give students experience with how teams work, and team members get acquainted with each other's Project Plans. Upon graduation, the teams begin to meet weekly in the new cities, as arranged before graduation. As placements shrink the teams, they become virtual teams that can be combined regardless of location.

If the school has an ongoing JSWT program sponsored by the alumni association in a destination city, the graduating students can be merged into those teams. This provides an array of benefits for all of the job hunters, including an expanded alumni network.

A one-year pilot of this type of program was conducted at Mount Holyoke College. Scott Brown and Cori Ashworth described it in the *Journal of the National Association of Colleges and Employers* (NACE) in May, 2009.

Option #2: On-campus JSWTs become virtual teams at graduation.

The on-campus portion of this kind of program is as above, but teams are limited to seven members. Then, at graduation, the on-campus teams become virtual teams, as described on page 58.

These teams will shrink as members find employment. Teams that shrink to three or fewer members each should be combined into larger teams. Team members should be cautioned from the outset that someone will be the last person hired, so that last person doesn't feel like a failure. This issue is less serious when the teams are professionally led.

Advanced Job Search Work Teams

When your team is problem–free and functioning well, you may want to take it to the next level by adding some of the suggestions on these pages. It's not a good idea to try to do these right away in a new team. But once you've got the basics under control, these are some additional areas to consider.

Be very cautious with the two items that add activities to the meeting. If you don't strictly control the time, they can take far more time than they're worth.

Making the most of the Two to Four Hour agreement requires very little meeting time and can produce great benefits. Subgroups and pairs working between meetings can practice skills, better educate themselves on search and solve more complex problems. These activities are arranged in the meetings or immediately after the meetings.

Examples of in-meeting and between-meeting activities include:

- **Networking with a minimum of meeting time.** In advanced teams, members often mention the names of their targets during progress reporting. Because members are highly familiar with each other's target lists, they can frequently volunteer information––or even introductions––to each other during the meeting.

  However, they never take much time to do that. It's nearly always, "I've got something for you on the company you just mentioned. Talk to me after the meeting." While observing a high-functioning team of 10 members, I once counted 17 of those brief interactions in a single meeting.

- **Conducting Project Plan reviews** outside of team meetings. Especially in a difficult job market, an essential part of effective job search is regular review of the Project Plan. Because it's personal to the individual, it must always be done outside of the meeting. Advanced teams have mechanisms for regularly doing this with each member who wants to.

  In a subgroup with a set time limit, a member makes a presentation of the evidence they have accumulated in their networking discussions, evidence that shows that their Project Plan is appropriate and effective – or that it may need improvement. The group then has a discussion of whether the Project Plan should be revised, and if so, how. Three reviews can usually be completed in a 60- to 90-minute meeting of three members.

- **Introducing existing members to new members.** When a new member joins a team, advanced teams will sometimes go around the table with 60-second introductions (using a time-keeper) of everyone in the room, using the well-rehearsed "elevator speech" that all job hunters should have. This is an opportunity for the new member to learn about existing members. Equally important, it's a chance for everyone to practice their speeches.

  This should definitely not be attempted until a team is highly competent with progress reports, and it's better not to mix it with progress reporting. Instead, go around the table twice, once with the introductions and then with the normal progress reporting.

When team members are effective at progress reports and elevator speeches, this is a great thing to do now and then. But if the team isn't highly effective at these, it can be a serious time-waster, taking much more than 12 minutes and becoming a diversion that reduces the effectiveness of the meeting.

- **Including a "job hunting resources" time in the meeting wrap-up.** In this brief section at the end of a meeting, members request information on needed resources or share information on existing resources. Examples include: the time and place of networking groups or talks, titles of job hunting books, job search software, relevant technology and useful websites.

  Maintain a tight time limit on this, with no discussion, to keep it to four minutes or less. Members wanting further information on a resource mentioned should talk to the knowledgeable person after the meeting.

- **Using numbers and ratios.** In advanced teams, members use observation of their own Progress Chart numbers as the basis for agenda items. For example, a member might say, "I notice that most of you have more favorable ratios of general networking conversations to Decision Maker conversations than I do. I'm at about 22 to one. Some of you are at 10 to one. What could someone do to improve their ratio?"

- **Interviewing practice sessions** between meetings are a high-value activity for subgroups between meetings. This is best done in groups of three team members, playing the roles of interviewer, job candidate, and observer.

  Use some of the standard interview questions found in interviewing books. Do not evaluate "body language," since that's hard for anyone except professional actors to change. Do not be too hard on the candidate. The idea is to give the candidate practice getting comfortable with verbalizing strengths and other information normally requested, in order to increase their effectiveness and confidence.

  The observer should tell the candidate the three things that were effective and worked well, and one specific suggestion for how to improve one of the areas covered. Remember that too much analysis and criticism can do more harm than good. The three team members rotate through the three roles.

- **Interview debriefing** is another high-value activity. This can be done in a meeting of two people, one who just had a job interview (and recorded notes on the entire event immediately after leaving the interview), and one who agrees to assist. It can be done on the phone or in person.

  The person who was interviewed talks through the entire interview in detail – quoting what was said as best they can — beginning to end. The two then discuss strong points, areas for improvement, and the content of a substantial post-interview written follow-up communication.

CHAPTER 6

Job Search Work Team Toolkit

This chapter contains samples all of the tools you need for a successful Job Search Work Team. Each tool is preceded by a page explaining its use. All of these tools have also been discussed in previous sections of this book.

You can remove the tools from the book or you can download them free of charge from my website, www.highlyeffectivejobsearch.com. I recommend the downloadable versions, since they're a little larger and have no page numbers on them. Here are the six tools:

TOOL	DEFINITION
JSWT Contract PAGE 67	The agreements signed by all team members. Without these six agreements, you cannot expect the team to produce the results we discussed in this book.
Job Search Progress Chart PAGE 73	The sheet that you use to record your progress tracking numbers each week.
Weekly Report tent card PAGE 77	A name tent that's used to display your key progress tracking numbers in each weekly meeting.
Reminder Card PAGE 83	A folded card that sets on the table in the team meeting room. It displays the six agreements of the JSWT Contract and the format of a progress report.
Optional Wall Chart PAGE 87	A large chart that can be posted on the wall and used as a substitute for the Weekly Report tent cards.
JSWT Final Report PAGE 91	A template for the report that you give to the team when you land a new job.

The JSWT Contract

We discussed this contract and its use on page 48. There is a sample copy of it on page 67.

The JSWT Contract is essential to the success of a Job Search Work Team. Without these six agreements, the group is not a JSWT, and there is no reason to expect it to provide the benefits of a JSWT.

When a new member joins a team, they should download a copy of the contract (or remove it from this book), take it to a team meeting and sign it. The signing is usually done at the conclusion of the first or second team meeting.

Some teams have all members initial the new member's contract, as a way of affirming that the agreement is between the new member and all other members, rather than between the member and the leader.

You may recall that the JSWT Declaration of Inter-Dependence listed the three principles on which the teams are based: Productive participation, mutual support and celebration of success. On the following page, there is a chart that shows how those principles are related to the six behaviors listed in the JSWT Contract.

Some team leaders briefly remind members of the principles, the contract or both at the beginning of each meeting. I recommend doing that whenever a visitor is present and whenever a new member signs the contract.

Team Principles and the JSWT Contract

This chart shows how the principles on which the team is founded are expressed in the behaviors that all team members agree to in the contract. The principles and meeting behaviors are both essential to the effectiveness of the team. And they help make the team – and your job search – more pleasant.

The Principles (Our Values)	The Agreements (Our Behaviors)
PRODUCTIVE PARTICIPATION: We fully, actively and enthusiastically participate in improving our own job searches and actively support others in doing the same. We value collaboration.	1. Attend/report 2. Two to four hours 4. Donuts and debriefing 5. Read three books 6. Follow the guidelines
MUTUAL SUPPORT: We see other job hunters as allies, and we assist them in the work of the search, offer personal support in good times and bad, and always respect their opinions and their individual ways of doing things.	2. Two to four hours 3. Respect 5. Read three books 6. Follow the guidelines
CELEBRATION OF SUCCESS: We celebrate new jobs and career advancement. We celebrate all of the small successes that lead to the large ones. We recognize and honor the effort that leads to these successes.	1. Attend/report 4. Donuts and debriefing

The JSWT Contract

1. Attend/report I agree to use the Job Search Progress Chart and the Weekly Report tent card. I will provide reports at every weekly team meeting without exception, whether I attend the meeting or not.

I will attend every meeting unless I have a personal emergency, an illness, an important family event or a job interview. If I have to miss a meeting for one of those reasons, I will give my report to another member who will read it to the team.

2. Two to four hours I agree to diligently seek opportunities to volunteer two to four hours of my time each week to assist one or more team members between meetings. I understand that I am not required to do anything that anyone asks of me, but I will do my best to find situations where I can honestly and comfortably assist someone. I will not exceed four hours per week, since my primary responsibility is my own job search.

3. Respect I agree to respect my fellow team members. The most important examples of this are: Take only my fair share of meeting time. Never attack or belittle anyone about anything. Arrive early for meetings, not merely on time. Resign in person at a regular meeting if leaving the team without a new job.

4. Donuts and debriefing When I land a new job, I agree to debrief the team by using the Final Report to the Team in its entirety — in person, in writing or both. I also agree to provide donuts, or some other snack food, at the team meeting immediately following my acceptance of a new job. If I am unable to attend the meeting, I will make arrangements with another team member to have that person deliver the Final Report and food on my behalf.

5. Three books I agree to read at least three job hunting books in the first 90 days of my team membership, one or more a month. I understand that reading *The Unwritten Rules of the Highly Effective Job Search* is strongly recommended.

6. Follow the guidelines I agree to follow the guidelines in the JSWT book, *Team Up! Find a Better Job Faster with a Job Search Work Team.*

I understand that keeping these six agreements is an essential part of making the Job Search Work Team effective for all members. If I ever neglect one of them, I would like someone to remind me about that, politely and privately. I understand that if I fail to keep these agreements, I may be asked to leave the team.

Your name (please print): _____ Date _____

Your Signature _____

The Job Search Progress Chart

You can download a copy at www.highlyeffectivejobsearch.com

The Progress Chart is essential to the success of a Job Search Work Team. Without progress tracking, the group is not a JSWT, and there is no reason to expect it to provide the benefits of a JSWT. The Progress Chart is a productivity tool that is useful for any job hunter, even without a team.

You can see a Progress Chart on page 73. Instructions for using them are on page 70. There is an example of a completed Progress Chart on page 71, so you can see what yours might look like at the end of a calendar month.

You can remove the Progress Chart from this book, or use the higher quality downloadable version. Whichever you choose, make some two-sided copies of it. Always be sure to take the chart for the current month to your team meeting every week. You'll need the information to complete your Weekly Report tent card, and may wish to refer to it during advisory panel discussions.

The Progress Chart is a two-sided document, so be sure to copy the second side on the back. That way, you'll always have the definitions of the chart's categories when you're using the chart.

Excel Version of the Job Search Progress Chart

You can download a copy at www.highlyeffectivejobsearch.com

Some team members prefer the Excel version of the Progress Chart, since it does the arithmetic for you. It's identical to the paper version. Please use whichever version is more convenient for you.

Job Search Progress Chart

(1) Use one Progress Chart for each month. Enter the dates of the four (or five) Mondays of the month in the "Week beginning on" line. Enter your weekly averages from last month in the first column, on the left.

(2) Track your activities from Monday through Sunday, add up the totals for each category and record those numbers on the Progress Chart at the end of the week. If you are a member of a Job Search Work Team that meets on a day other than Monday, adjust steps one and two accordingly.

(3) Record your numbers for each week in the column for that date. Check the definitions of the categories on the back of the Progress Chart to understand exactly what you are counting in each of the categories.

(4) At the end of the last week on your chart, add up the totals for each row and record those totals in the "Total for the month" column.

(5) Divide each of those totals by the number of weeks your chart covers, and record that number in the "Average per week" box next to the "Total" box. Averages below 10 are rounded to the nearest tenth, i.e. 1.2, 1.7, 2.4, etc. Averages of 10 or more are rounded to the nearest whole number, with no decimals.

 (6) Please note that the box in the lower right hand corner is the total number of interviews for your entire search, not an average, since most job hunters have many weeks without interviews. Focus your efforts on initial Decision Maker conversations, since you can control those. Sooner or later those informal conversations will lead to interviews.

(7) When giving the "Numbers" section of your verbal progress report (see page 46) in the team meeting, mention your average per week for last month along with your number for the current week in each of the ten categories. Mention any interviews as part of the "Highlights" section of your report. You will also record most of these numbers on your JSWT Weekly Report tent card (see page 77).

(8) When a team member expects to miss a meeting, that team member transmits the usual weekly progress report to another member who gives the verbal report for them, as discussed in "Attend/Report" on page 48.

Your name **Orville Pierson**   Date your search began **4/21**

JOB SEARCH PROGRESS CHART

For the month: (circle one) Jan Feb Mar Apr May Jun Jul (Aug) Sep Oct Nov Dec

AVERAGE per week last month	Week beginning on:	8/4 (date)	8/11 (date)	8/18 (date)	8/25 (date)	(date)	TOTAL for the month	AVERAGE per week this month
32	TOTAL HOURS in job search this week	35	25	38	27		125	31

EMPLOYER CONTACTS

3.7	JOB POSTINGS - # you responded to	4	7	1	5		17	4.3
1.9	DIRECT EMPLOYER CONTACT - initial	1	2	—	3		6	1.5
8.1	DIRECT EMPLOYER CONTACT – follow-up	10	6	—	4		20	5.0

JOB SEARCH CONVERSATIONS

29	GEN'L NETWORK- search conversations with anyone at all	35	28	24	34		121	30
0.8	TARGET MISC.- conversations with misc. insiders	2	1	1	—		4	1.0
1.7	TARGET PEER- conversations with insiders at your level	3	3	—	1		7	1.8
1.6	DECISION MAKER (& above)- initial contact only	3	2	1	2		8	2.0
4.0	DECISION MAKER (& above)- follow-up contacts with DM's	4	3	6	6		19	4.8
37	TOTAL conversations for the week-Total the five categories above	47	37	32	43		159	40

JOB INTERVIEWS

						TOTAL for the month	TOTAL for entire search
# of Decision Maker conversations that were job interviews	—	—	1	—		1	3

Instructions for using this Job Search Progress Chart are on page 70 of *Team Up! Find a Better Job Faster with a Job Search Work Team*. Definitions of the categories used in the second column from the left are on the other side of this sheet.

A Completed Job Search Progress Chart

This is an example of a chart that has been used for a full calendar month, so you can see how it's done. The numbers in the last column on the right side of this chart will be copied into the first (left-hand) column of the next month's chart.

Job Search Progress Chart: Definitions of Categories

TOTAL HOURS in job search this week
The total number of hours you spent in job hunting in the last seven days, including research, educating yourself on effective job hunting, talking to people, applying to posted jobs, administration, e-mailing, and *everything* else you did in your search, whether or not you regarded those activities as productive or successful.

EMPLOYER CONTACTS

JOB POSTINGS - # you responded to
The total number of individual job postings that you responded to, regardless of where they appeared.

DIRECT EMPLOYER CONTACT – initial
The total number of employers you contacted without an introduction or posting, either by phone (cold calling) or by e-mail/snail mail (direct mail). This category includes only the first contact with each. Voicemails, e-mails and letters with no response are all counted. Completed job applications count as contacts here. Making an initial contact with a staffing or search firm is counted here, since they are an outsourced part of the employer's staffing function. If you actually had a conversation with someone, count it in JOB SEARCH CONVERSATIONS, below.

DIRECT EMPLOYER CONTACT – follow-up
The total number of employers you attempted to follow-up with by phone or in writing, after an initial cold call or direct mail contact. This includes only second and successive contacts. Voicemails, e-mails and letters with no response are all counted. If you actually had a conversation with someone, count it in JOB SEARCH CONVERSATIONS, below. Please note: this is follow-up with Decision Makers that you have NOT spoken with.

JOB SEARCH CONVERSATIONS

GEN'L NETWORK- job search conversations with anyone not at a targeted organization
The total number of job search related conversations you had with anyone who is not currently employed in one of your target organizations. Successive conversations with the same person are all counted here, as are two-way conversations with staffing or search firms.

TARGET MISC.- conversations with misc. insiders
Conversations with anyone inside a targeted organization who is not a peer or Decision Maker.

TARGET PEER- conversations with insiders at your level
Conversations with anyone inside a targeted organization who is more or less at your level.

DECISION MAKER (& above)- initial contact only
Conversations of any length – in person or on the phone — with a person who could be your next boss, or with that person's boss or anyone above them. Count only the first conversation with that person in this category. Count all successive contacts in the follow-up category, so that this number is the number of *different* Decision Makers you've talked to. An e-mail exchange in which each party sends three or more e-mails is counted as one conversation.

DECISION MAKER (& above)- follow-up contacts
This is where you count all successive contacts with Decision Makers contacted above. Research shows that job hunters who re-contact each and every Decision Maker every two to four weeks find jobs more quickly than those who do not do this. These follow-up contacts do not need to be conversations. While conversations are much better if you can politely get them, these can also be contacts with no response, just like Direct Employer follow-ups.

JOB INTERVIEWS

# of Decision Maker conversations that were job interviews
This is a sub-category of Decision Maker contacts, so any actual job interview – no matter how you got it — is counted in both categories. Initial post-interview follow-up is usually in writing and should be carefully thought out. If you are not selected, continue to do Decision Maker follow-up as above. You were a finalist. They liked you. Let them off the hook for not selecting you. Do not put them on the defensive. Continue to tell them how you would still like to work there, should another opportunity arise. This is just as important as other follow-up.

Your name _____ Date your search began _____

JOB SEARCH PROGRESS CHART

For the month: (circle one) Jan Feb Mar Apr May Jun Jul Aug Sep Oct Nov Dec

AVERAGE per week last month	Week beginning on:	____ (date)	____ (date)	____ (date)	____ (date)	____ (date)	TOTAL for the month	AVERAGE per week this month
	TOTAL HOURS in job search this week							

EMPLOYER CONTACTS

	JOB POSTINGS - # you responded to							
	DIRECT EMPLOYER CONTACT - initial							
	DIRECT EMPLOYER CONTACT – follow-up							

JOB SEARCH CONVERSATIONS

	GEN'L NETWORK- search conversations with anyone at all							
	TARGET MISC.- conversations with misc. insiders							
	TARGET PEER- conversations with insiders at your level							
	DECISION MAKER (& above)- initial contact only							
	DECISION MAKER (& above)- follow-up contacts with DM's							
	TOTAL conversations for the week-Total the five categories above							

JOB INTERVIEWS

	TOTAL for the month	TOTAL for entire search

	# of Decision Maker conversations that were job interviews							

Instructions for using this Job Search Progress Chart are on page 70 of *Team Up! Find a Better Job Faster with a Job Search Work Team*. Definitions of the categories used in the second column from the left are on the other side of this sheet.

Job Search Progress Chart: Definitions of Categories

TOTAL HOURS in job search this week
The total number of hours you spent in job hunting in the last seven days, including research, educating yourself on effective job hunting, talking to people, applying to posted jobs, administration, e-mailing, and *everything* else you did in your search, whether or not you regarded those activities as productive or successful.

EMPLOYER CONTACTS

JOB POSTINGS - # you responded to
The total number of individual job postings that you responded to, regardless of where they appeared.

DIRECT EMPLOYER CONTACT – initial
The total number of employers you contacted without an introduction or posting, either by phone (cold calling) or by e-mail/snail mail (direct mail). This category includes only the first contact with each. Voicemails, e-mails and letters with no response are all counted. Completed job applications count as contacts here. Making an initial contact with a staffing or search firm is counted here, since they are an outsourced part of the employer's staffing function. If you actually had a conversation with someone, count it in JOB SEARCH CONVERSATIONS, below.

DIRECT EMPLOYER CONTACT – follow-up
The total number of employers you attempted to follow-up with by phone or in writing, after an initial cold call or direct mail contact. This includes only second and successive contacts. Voicemails, e-mails and letters with no response are all counted. If you actually had a conversation with someone, count it in JOB SEARCH CONVERSATIONS, below. Please note: this is follow-up with Decision Makers that you have NOT spoken with.

JOB SEARCH CONVERSATIONS

GEN'L NETWORK- job search conversations with anyone not at a targeted organization
The total number of job search related conversations you had with anyone who is not currently employed in one of your target organizations. Successive conversations with the same person are all counted here, as are two-way conversations with staffing or search firms.

TARGET MISC.- conversations with misc. insiders
Conversations with anyone inside a targeted organization who is not a peer or Decision Maker.

TARGET PEER- conversations with insiders at your level
Conversations with anyone inside a targeted organization who is more or less at your level.

DECISION MAKER (& above)- initial contact only
Conversations of any length – in person or on the phone — with a person who could be your next boss, or with that person's boss or anyone above them. Count only the first conversation with that person in this category. Count all successive contacts in the follow-up category, so that this number is the number of *different* Decision Makers you've talked to. An e-mail exchange in which each party sends three or more e-mails is counted as one conversation.

DECISION MAKER (& above)- follow-up contacts
This is where you count all successive contacts with Decision Makers contacted above. Research shows that job hunters who re-contact each and every Decision Maker every two to four weeks find jobs more quickly than those who do not do this. These follow-up contacts do not need to be conversations. While conversations are much better if you can politely get them, these can also be contacts with no response, just like Direct Employer follow-ups.

JOB INTERVIEWS

# of Decision Maker conversations that were job interviews
This is a sub-category of Decision Maker contacts, so any actual job interview – no matter how you got it — is counted in both categories. Initial post-interview follow-up is usually in writing and should be carefully thought out. If you are not selected, continue to do Decision Maker follow-up as above. You were a finalist. They liked you. Let them off the hook for not selecting you. Do not put them on the defensive. Continue to tell them how you would still like to work there, should another opportunity arise. This is just as important as other follow-up.

The JSWT Weekly Report
Tent Card

You can download a copy at www.highlyeffectivejobsearch.com

Every team member uses a Weekly Report tent card in every meeting. They look like a name tent, but they display the key Progress Report numbers as well as your name. And as we've discussed, it's important for everyone to know everyone else's progress reporting numbers. The Weekly Report tent cards also make it easier for new members to learn everyone's name.

So before each meeting, each member completes a Weekly Report tent card and sets it on the table in front of them. When giving the your verbal progress report, it's useful to hold the card up to make sure everyone can see your numbers. It then remains on the table in front of you for the rest of the meeting.

If there is ever a team member who misses a meeting and does not send in a report, someone contacts them, as discussed on pages 50 and 54. At the next meeting, that member fills in two panels of the Weekly Report, one for each week. During the report, that person displays first one panel of the Weekly Report, then the other, so the team can clearly see the progress report "Numbers" for each of the two weeks.

Instructions for using the JSWT Weekly Report tent cards are on the next page. A completed sample of a JSWT Weekly Report tent card appears on page 77.

The optional Wall Chart can be used instead of the Weekly Report tent cards. There is never a need to use both. Each team selects the one that works best for them, and then uses that one consistently.

The JSWT Weekly Report
Tent Card

Download a Weekly Report tent card from www.highlyeffectivejobsearch.com or remove the copy from this book. It's best to photocopy them onto 65 lb. paper (light card stock), but ordinary paper can be used. Fold the report along the dotted line to make a tent card that looks like the illustration below.

Because each tent card has four panels, two on the outside and two on the inside, each card can be used for four weeks.

Record the current week's numbers and averages from your Progress Chart on a JSWT Weekly Report name tent at each meeting, as shown in the sample on page 77.

Use markers or crayons to fill in the blanks on the Weekly Report. With markers, take care that they do not bleed through the paper to the surface below. Use one color for "this week" and another color for "average per week last month" and use a dash (-) instead of a zero. Using two colors makes it easier for others to read the numbers.

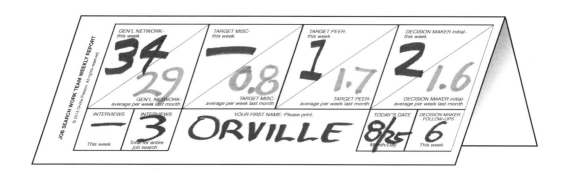

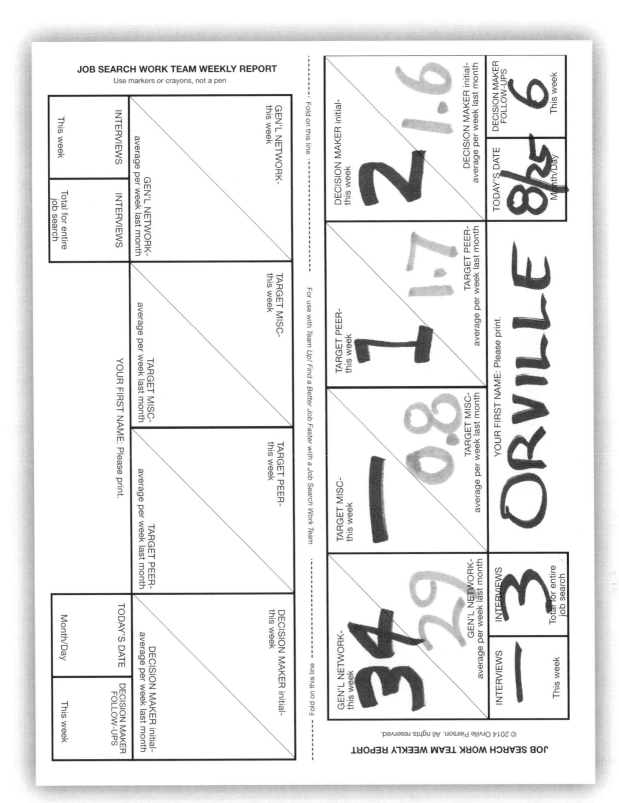

A Completed Weekly Report Tent Card

This is an example of a Weekly Report prepared for use in a meeting. The numbers used in this sample are taken from the week labeled 8/25 in the sample JSWT Progress Chart on page 71.

JOB SEARCH WORK TEAM WEEKLY REPORT

Use markers or crayons, not a pen

Fold on this line

For use with *Team Up! Find a Better Job Faster with a Job Search Work Team*

GEN'L NETWORK- this week

GEN'L NETWORK- average per week last month

TARGET MISC- this week

TARGET MISC- average per week last month

TARGET PEER- this week

TARGET PEER- average per week last month

DECISION MAKER initial- this week

DECISION MAKER initial- average per week last month

INTERVIEWS

INTERVIEWS

This week

Total for entire job search

YOUR FIRST NAME: Please print.

TODAY'S DATE

Month/Day

This week

DECISION MAKER FOLLOW-UPS

DECISION MAKER initial- this week

DECISION MAKER initial- average per week last month

TARGET PEER- this week

TARGET PEER- average per week last month

TARGET MISC- this week

TARGET MISC- average per week last month

GEN'L NETWORK- this week

GEN'L NETWORK- average per week last month

INTERVIEWS

INTERVIEWS

This week

Total for entire job search

YOUR FIRST NAME: Please print.

TODAY'S DATE

Month/Day

This week

DECISION MAKER FOLLOW-UPS

Fold on this line

JOB SEARCH WORK TEAM WEEKLY REPORT

JOB SEARCH WORK TEAM WEEKLY REPORT
Use markers or crayons, not a pen

GEN'L NETWORK-
this week

GEN'L NETWORK-
average per week last month

INTERVIEWS

INTERVIEWS

This week

Total for entire job search

TARGET MISC-
this week

TARGET MISC-
average per week last month

TARGET PEER-
this week

TARGET PEER-
average per week last month

YOUR FIRST NAME: Please print.

DECISION MAKER initial-
this week

DECISION MAKER initial-
average per week last month

TODAY'S DATE

DECISION MAKER FOLLOW-UPS

Month/Day

This week

Fold on this line

For use with *Team Up! Find a Better Job Faster with a Job Search Work Team*

DECISION MAKER initial-
this week

DECISION MAKER initial-
average per week last month

TODAY'S DATE

DECISION MAKER FOLLOW-UPS

Month/Day

This week

TARGET PEER-
this week

TARGET PEER-
average per week last month

TARGET MISC-
this week

TARGET MISC-
average per week last month

YOUR FIRST NAME: Please print.

GEN'L NETWORK-
this week

GEN'L NETWORK-
average per week last month

INTERVIEWS

INTERVIEWS

This week

Total for entire job search

Fold on this line

JOB SEARCH WORK TEAM WEEKLY REPORT

Use markers or crayons, not a pen

GEN'L NETWORK- this week

GEN'L NETWORK- average per week last month

INTERVIEWS

INTERVIEWS

This week

Total for entire job search

TARGET MISC- this week

TARGET MISC- average per week last month

TARGET PEER- this week

TARGET PEER- average per week last month

YOUR FIRST NAME: Please print.

DECISION MAKER initial- this week

DECISION MAKER initial- average per week last month

TODAY'S DATE

Month/Day

DECISION MAKER FOLLOW-UPS

This week

Fold on this line

For use with Team Up! Find a Better Job Faster with a Job Search Work Team

Fold on this line

DECISION MAKER initial- this week

DECISION MAKER initial- average per week last month

DECISION MAKER FOLLOW-UPS

This week

TODAY'S DATE

Month/Day

TARGET PEER- this week

TARGET PEER- average per week last month

TARGET MISC- this week

TARGET MISC- average per week last month

YOUR FIRST NAME: Please print.

GEN'L NETWORK- this week

GEN'L NETWORK- average per week last month

INTERVIEWS

INTERVIEWS

Total for entire job search

This week

JOB SEARCH WORK TEAM WEEKLY REPORT

The JSWT Reminder Card

The Reminder Card on the following page can be removed from this book or downloaded from www.highlyeffectivejobsearch.com, then folded into a two-panel card that you can set on the table in a JSWT meeting.

Having a Reminder Card on the table at every meeting reminds team members of the four elements of a Progress Report. New members can use this as a guide when giving their report.

It also reminds people of the six agreements they made in the JSWT Contract. Remembering these agreements is essential to team success.

To use the card, fold it on the three dotted lines. Then glue or tape the tab to the back of the JSWT Contract panel. This creates a permanent card like the one in the illustration below, one your team can use week after week.

If you photocopy the downloaded card onto 65 lb. paper (light card stock), you will have a more durable version.

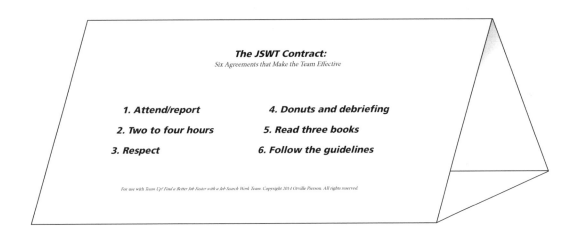

The JSWT Contract:
Six Agreements that Make the Team Effective

1. **Attend/report**   4. **Donuts and debriefing**

2. **Two to four hours**   5. **Read three books**

3. **Respect**   6. **Follow the guidelines**

For use with Team Up! Find a Better Job Faster with a Job Search Work Team. Copyright 2014 Orville Pierson. All rights reserved.

The JSWT Contract:
Six Agreements that Make the Team Effective

1. **Attend/report**

2. **Two to four hours**

3. **Respect**

4. **Donuts and debriefing**

5. **Read three books**

6. **Follow the guidelines**

------------------------------ FOLD ON THIS LINE ------------------------------

Job Search Progress Report
Three minutes per person

1. Your numbers. Read the current week's numbers — paired with last month's averages — from your Progress Chart, without comment or explanation. Hold up your Weekly Report tent card so members can see the numbers in writing. This can be done in 30 seconds.

2. Three highlights of your week in job search. Mention the three best things that you did or that happened to you in job hunting in the last seven days. These could include: a major breakthrough; a small step in the right direction; a problem solved; or a "gift from God," something useful that came your way with no effort on your part.

3. Three priorities for the coming week. Refer to your Project Plan and Target List. Your priorities should usually include pursuit of several targeted organizations where you have so far made little or no progress. Mention the names of those organizations.

4. Your agenda item is an immediate and practical job search issue, phrased as a question. It could be about something that did not go well in your job search in the last seven days or how to best approach something you're planning for the next week.

------------------------------ FOLD ON THIS LINE ------------------------------

------------------------------ FOLD ON THIS LINE ------------------------------

TAPE OR GLUE THIS TAB TO THE BACK OF THE JSWT CONTRACT PANEL.

Optional Wall Chart

This chart must be at least 26" wide by 30" high.

The wall chart on page 87 is an alternative to the Weekly Report tent card. Use whichever is more convenient for your team. There is never a need to use both. Each team selects the one that works best for them, and then uses that one consistently.

If your team decides to use the optional wall chart instead of the Weekly Report tent card, download the pdf from www.highlyeffectivejobsearch.com and have a copy shop print very large copies for you. Your team will use one copy at each weekly meeting, so make plenty of copies.

The wall chart needs to be easily seen by everyone sitting at the meeting table, so 26 inches wide by 30 inches high is a minimum size. If you plan to use markers, be sure the paper is thick enough that the marker ink does not bleed through and stain the wall. With thinner paper, use crayons.

Before the meeting, the first names of team members are written in the wide horizontal spaces in the left hand column. The leader then records each member's numbers in the ten boxes to the right of their name. These are the same numbers that would be recorded on the Weekly Report tent cards if your team used them. Each person's numbers are filled in as they give the numerical part of their progress report. The leader uses one color for last month's averages, and a different color for this week's numbers.

If you want to make a chart like this, rather than have it done at a copy shop, draw 2-inch squares on a flipchart page and make the rest like the illustration on the next page.

A permanent whiteboard version

An alternative to paper wall charts is a whiteboard with permanently painted lines. The numbers can be erased and replaced each week. Names can be erased and replaced as members find jobs.

The Optional JSWT Wall Chart

May be used instead of Weekly Report tent cards.

Download the pdf from www.highlyeffectivejobsearch.com and have a copy shop print it for you. To be seen by all team members, it must be much larger than shown below, at least 26 inches wide by 30 inches high.

Job Search Work Team Wall Chart

DATE:

TEAM NAME:

	General Network		Target Misc.		Target Peer		Decision Maker Initial		DECISION MAKER F/U THIS WEEK	INTERVIEWS TOTAL FOR ENTIRE SEARCH
	THIS WEEK	AVERAGE	THIS WEEK	AVERAGE	THIS WEEK	AVERAGE	THIS WEEK	AVERAGE		
	(COLOR A)	(COLOR B)	(COLOR A)	(COLOR B)	(COLOR A)	(COLOR B)	(COLOR A)	(COLOR B)	(COLOR A)	(COLOR B)
NAME:										
NAME:										
NAME:										
NAME:										
NAME:										
NAME:										
NAME:										
NAME:										
NAME:										
NAME:										
NAME:										
NAME:										

Final Report to the Team

You can download a copy at www.highlyeffectivejobsearch.com

Completing this Final Report is one of the most important services a team member can perform for the team. It shows everyone exactly what a successful job search looks like: how much effort it requires, the stages a job hunter goes through and the key factors contributing to success.

It's useful for job hunters to see a number of these Final Reports, because there are elements of a job search that are common to all job hunters, as well as ways each search is unique. So the more Final Reports you see, the more you learn.

The report is particularly meaningful to those who have witnessed the team member's search on a week-to-week basis. But it's an excellent learning device for any job hunter – and one I like to use as part of training career professionals.

It's useful for teams to collect all written Final Reports and make them available to new members who want to read them. Teams that have their own meeting space sometimes have a chart on the wall – a kind of Honor Roll of successful members. It includes the names of team members who have landed, along with a numerical progress summary of the entire search (Item #2 in the Final Report) for each.

Completing this Final Report is one of the agreements each team member makes in the JSWT Contract. When you land a job, use the following page as a guide for preparing your report.

Final Report to the Team

You can download a copy in Word at www.highlyeffectivejobsearch.com

One of the agreements you made in the JSWT Contract is to debrief your Job Search Work Team on your entire job search project when you land a new job. Please use this outline to prepare a verbal or written report. In giving this report verbally, plan for a 10-minute presentation to the team. If you are starting your new job immediately and can't give the report in person, please write it up so a teammate can give the report for you.

1. Your name, team name and today's date.

2. Your new job. Give a brief description of your new position and organization. Please mention the two or three things about the job or the organization that you like best, those that were most important in your decision to accept the job offer.

3. Overall progress summary. Use your Progress Charts to calculate the grand totals for each of the following categories. If the demands of transitioning into your new job do not permit you to complete this, please give all of your Progress Charts to another team member and ask them to do the totals. Or make estimates based on monthly averages. Each of the numbers below is a grand total for your entire job search, beginning to end. You can record these on a blank Progress Chart, or simply list them on paper.

- TOTAL NUMBER OF WEEKS IN YOUR JOB SEARCH
- TOTAL HOURS in your entire job search
- TOTAL JOB POSTINGS - # you responded to
- TOTAL DIRECT EMPLOYER CONTACT – initial
- TOTAL DIRECT EMPLOYER CONTACT – follow-up
- TOTAL GEN'L NETWORK- search conversations with anyone at all
- TOTAL TARGET MISC.- conversations with misc. insiders
- TOTAL TARGET PEER- conversations with insiders at your level
- TOTAL DECISION MAKER (& above)- initial contact only
- TOTAL DECISION MAKER (& above)- follow-up contacts with Decision Makers
- TOTAL JOB INTERVIEWS - # of Decision Maker conversations that were job interviews

4. The story of your job search. Please briefly tell the story of your entire search. In doing so, divide your job search into phases or chapters, and give each of those a descriptive title. In giving your report, name each of the chapters and give a brief description of what happened in each.

5. Strategy. As your job search proceeded, did you modify your Project Plan (i.e. your Professional Objective, Core Message or Target Market criteria)? If so, when and why?

6. Success factors. What were the most important factors in your success? How did the team (or individual teammates) help you succeed?

7. Advice. Now that you have successfully completed your job search, what advice would you give to your teammates who are still in job search? Please keep this to one sentence.

For use with *Team Up! Find a Better Job Faster with a Job Search Work Team*.
Copyright 2014 Orville Pierson. All rights reserved.

Job Search Work Team Summary

The infographic on the next two pages summarizes the entire Job Search Work Team process. This quick overview lets you see at a glance how all the pieces you just read about fit together.

Job Search Work Teams

1

Preparation

Your Project Plan:
- Professional Objective
- Target Market
- Core Message

Your Target List

Your resume. . .

. . . and all other preparation

2

The JSWT Contract

1. **Attend/report**
2. **Two to four hours**
3. **Respect other team members**
4. **Donuts and debriefing**
5. **Three books**
6. **Follow the guidelines**

3

Your Progress Chart

Use these progress measurements:

1. **The number of hours devoted to job search this week**

2. **The number of employer contacts this week:**
   - Job postings - # you responded to
   - Direct employer contact – initial
   - Direct employer contact – follow-up

3. **The number of informal job search conversations this week:**
   - General network
   - Target misc.
   - Target peer
   - Decision maker (& above)- initial
   - Decision maker (& above)- follow-up

4. **The total number of job interviews in your search so far**

4

The Team Meeting

Each weekly meeting includes:

1. Preparation of Weekly Reports

2. **Progress reporting** (3 minutes per person)
    - Your Progress Chart numbers
    - Three highlights
    - Three priorities
    - Your agenda item (optional)

3. **Agenda creation** (4 minutes)

4. **Advisory panel discussion of agenda items** (approximately 85 minutes)

5. **Meeting wrap-up** (0 to 4 minutes)

6. **Optional post-meeting discussions**

5

Land a Job!

6

Final Report to the Team

1. Your name, team, date
2. Your new job
3. Overall progress summary
4. The story of your job search
5. Your strategy
6. Success factors
7. Your advice to the team

7

Start Your New Job!

CHAPTER SEVEN

Your Personal Job Hunting Program

This is the last chapter of the book.

But maybe it's the first chapter of your job search. So I'd like to talk to you about shaping everything we've discussed into a personal job hunting program for you – a program that will give you the best chances of finding a really great job in the shortest possible time.

As someone who has designed a lot of job hunting programs, I know that they have two important parts. The first part is about skills and initial learning. You need to understand job search — how to prepare for it and how to do it.

So some education is useful at the outset. Most job hunters benefit from some instruction, based on a good strong skills curriculum. In Chapter 4, we talked about how career professionals do this with career counseling and workshops.

The second part of a strong program is what you just finished reading about: implementation of a highly effective search with the support of a team.

In this chapter, we'll talk about how to put those two parts together into the best possible program for you. I'll show you what an expensive top-of-the-line, professionally led program looks like. And I'll show you options for a great personal program for you, at little or no cost. Let's start by taking a quick look at the first part, job search skills.

The job hunting skills curriculum

Over the years, some things in job hunting have changed a lot, and some not so much. The core job hunting skills are an example of the latter. Most job hunting books and most job hunting instruction on the Internet focus on one or more of these skills – or one part of one of them. But to plan and implement a good strong program, you need to take a look at all of them.

To conduct an effective search, you need to learn or polish about a dozen skills. It's like any project you don't do very often – if you take the time to learn a few things at the outset, it all goes faster and better.

Some of those skills are things you use all the time and may already be good at. Others are unique to job hunting. And some are combinations of the two. You may already be good at networking, for example, but how it's used in job hunting is different, so you may still have some things to learn. Or you may be a power-user of LinkedIn or other social networking sites. But you still need to see how to best integrate them into your overall job hunting program.

The Job Hunting Skills Curriculum

Self assessment

Project Plan

- Professional Objective

- Target Market and Target List

- Core Message communications, including resume

The Seven Search Techniques

1. Walking in unannounced

2. Cold calling on the phone

3. Direct written contact

4. Completing applications

5. Responding to job postings

6. Using recruiters and staffing firms

7. Networking

Interviewing

Salary Negotiations

In job hunting, the skills are not complicated. Most people can learn them by reading a few well-chosen books. But it helps to think of them as a program or a curriculum, so you can learn them in an organized way — and not miss anything important.

Self assessment and career decisions

The original set of job hunting skills––which is still important today––begins with self assessment. This means examining your interests, skills, and values to decide what kind of work you want to pursue and clearly enumerating your personal and professional strengths.

This self-assessment work is particularly important for those who are just beginning their careers or considering making a big career change. But it's useful for everyone, to fine tune their choices on career direction. It's an activity that is included in most programs, sometimes called, "Know Yourself." It's an internal process, one that can be helped along by a good career counselor, and perhaps the use of some psychological instruments. But it can also be done by reading and talking with knowledgeable friends and acquaintances.

However, no matter what assistance you have, this is still *self* assessment. It's about your career and your life. Others can help you be more objective, but you still need to do it for yourself.

Project Plan

After self assessment, the curriculum moves on to deciding exactly what kind of work you're looking for, and expressing that as your Professional Objective. Then it moves to defining a Target Market, and making a Target List of the group of employers you'll pursue. And then to communications planning, determining the Core Message you'll use to communicate with that particular group of employers.

Communications planning also involves composing accomplishment stories that illustrate your personal and professional strengths. These stories are very useful in interviewing. And some of them are included in your resume.

Along with the resume, job hunters need a brief verbal presentation of their background that's often called an "elevator speech." The two of those and your LinkedIn profile all need to convey the same Core Message about what you have to offer employers. And they need to include the key-words that employers are likely to use in search-ing for you.

All of this is what I like to call your Project Plan. The Target Market and Target List part are a more recent evolution of the job hunting curriculum, based on the business discipline of marketing. Some books and websites do not yet include it.

Once that preparation work is done, the next sec-tion of the skills curriculum involves job search techniques and the best ways to use them.

The seven search techniques

These search techniques can also be called inter-view-getting methods. There are only seven. Most job hunters need to use some or all of them, effec-tively and persistently for many weeks. The seven skills are: walking in, cold calling, direct written contact, completing applications, responding to postings, using recruiters, and networking. You're most likely to find your next job by using one of the last three. But any of the last six could be important for salaried job hunters.

Because it is known to be the most generally useful of the seven, networking is a major piece of the skills curriculum of any strong job hunting program. Job hunters need to understand how it works in job search, what to say and not say, and how to use social networking websites as part of the process. Because it's so important to find effective and comfortable ways to do this, I wrote an entire book on it, *Highly Effective Networking: Meet the Right People and Find A Great Job*.

Interviewing and salary negotiations

The last piece of the program is usually interview-ing and salary negotiations, what to say and when. And what to avoid saying, and how to do that.

There are entire books on interviewing, some of which include salary negotiations. It's a good idea to read one of those sooner rather than later, because you simply don't know when your next interview opportunity will pop up.

It's also a very good idea to practice interviewing, from time-to-time –– starting now. When you get a call inviting you to a job interview, you may not have a lot of time to prepare. And you may need

---

To conduct an effective search, you need to learn or polish about a dozen skills.

---

some of that time to research the organization and its people. Smart job hunters set up regular interview practice sessions with members of their teams, a professional career coach, or other knowledgeable people.

A professionally led program

- A professional career coach

- A comprehensive workshop

- Numerical progress measurements

- Job Search Work Team

Job hunting skills: necessary but not sufficient

This skills curriculum – from self assessment all the way though to salary negotiations — is sometimes taught in the classroom by a career professional. But it can also be learned by reading books. What's important is that you learn these basic skills as early in your search as possible – and that you learn all of them, not just a few. Then, as you proceed with a search, you go deeper into the learning as you put it all to work in the real world.

For many years, it was believed that teaching this curriculum was all that was needed to make job hunters successful. And for a time, I believed that myself.

But the more I learned about job search assistance, the more certain I was that job hunting skills were necessary, but not sufficient, for a truly effective job search. Success requires more than just knowing the skills.

Job hunters who have learned these basics certainly have an advantage, but there's more to it. The learning has to be put to work, week after

week. In doing that, job hunters need to overcome the barriers to productivity that we looked at in Chapter 3. And the whole thing goes better if it's a well-planned program.

This kind of well-planned program is what you get in those expensive, executive level outplacements programs. They are all professionally led, of course, usually by people with many years of experience.

A professionally led program

A comprehensive workshop covering the entire skills curriculum is often the first event in a professionally led program. The workshop can be in a classroom, a webinar, or a series of e-learning courses. After the workshop, a career counselor works with you on the initial self-assessment, career planning and preparation of communications. Next, a career consultant assists you in determining your Target Market, researching an initial Target List and putting that together with the rest of your Project Plan. You'd have a career coach standing by to work with you on interviewing and salary negotiations.

And of course, you'd be using the Seven Search Techniques, along with numerical progress measurements in a Job Search Work Team, probably led by that same career coach. This kind of professionally led program combines the skills curriculum with everything else you read in this book. And yes, the counselor, consultant and coach could all be rolled into one experienced career professional, someone with all of those skills.

Top-of-the-line executive programs like this are offered by outplacement companies, but usually not to the general public. They're sold to organizations who purchase them for people they let go. Sometimes elements of a program like this are offered to the public by nonprofits, with or without a modest fee attached.

Theoretically, you could assemble a professionally led program like this for yourself. You might have to replace the workshop with books and career coaching, since it's difficult to find a well-designed, comprehensive job search assistance workshop that's available to the general public.

But the big obstacle is the cost. Career professionals usually charge $50 to $250 per hour. Adding that to the cost of renting space for meetings, you could pay thousands of dollars for a program like this, which is what the outplacement companies charge for it.

If you decide to go this way, please select your coach carefully, and pay for services an hour at a time, so you can change coaches if you want to.

But before you rush out and spend a lot of money, let's look at the alternatives.

Your personal program, at little or no cost

You can assemble a similar program for yourself at a much lower cost — or no cost at all. Granted, it wouldn't be the ideal program outlined above, since it wouldn't have a professional career coach. But it would be entirely adequate and would make your job search more effective, more comfortable and faster.

You would need to find a free meeting place, a coffee shop or restaurant perhaps, or a church basement or library. You would need to assemble Job Search Work Team members and they would need to read this book. Without a professional coach or a workshop, it is particularly important that all members of your team read some additional job hunting books.

You could use library books or have the team form its own little library, with each person con-

A personal program with a member-led team

- A number of good job hunting books

- Numerical progress measurements

- Job Search Work Team

tributing a book or two so everyone could borrow them for free. Then your program might look like the one at the bottom of page 101.

A personal program with a member-led team

In this kind of program, you replace the workshop with some good job hunting books and then use numerical progress measurements in a Job Search Work Team where team members are advisors to each other, in the meeting and outside of it.

Your teammates will assist you with your self-assessment and Project Plan, providing some objective feedback and advice in one-to-one meetings or in small groups – as you saw in the JSWT Manual. Team members also assist each other in learning and practicing interviewing and salary negotiations.

By the time you're interviewing, you'll know exactly which team member (or team alum) you want to go to for advice. And of course, the main topics of discussion at most team meetings are the seven search techniques. So everyone has an advisory panel on how to best handle the day-to-day search activities.

All of this adds up to the fact that your Job Search Work Team can cover all of the skill areas a career professional would assist you with. The advice and assistance might not be as sharp and concise, but it will be much less expensive.

A hybrid program

And here's one more possibility: a combination of elements. Some nonprofits and religious communities offer professionally led programs at little or no cost. You may be able to attend workshops and get access to counseling, coaching, and resume-writing assistance at one of those. You can combine parts of various programs, if one organization doesn't have it all.

Or you could pay for a few hours of professional coaching now and then to supplement your member-led team. You would then be using the coach like you might use a golf pro if you noticed that too many of your drives were landing on the wrong fairway, and you and your golfing partners couldn't figure out why. If you and your team are not able to solve an important job search problem, an hour or two with a career coach might be well worth the cost.

Four recommendations:

1. Use a professional coach if possible

2. Read several job hunting books, then use the Internet

3. Use numerical progress tracking

4. Use a Job Search Work Team — or arrange some other regular, objective support for yourself

Career coaches are available on an hourly basis

Four recommendations

I'd like to wrap up this book by offering four recommendations to help you put together a personal program to manage your search project. Here are the four:

1. Use a professional coach if possible

This can help you get the preparation for your job search (resume writing, interview practice, LinkedIn profile, etc.) done more quickly and more effectively. It's a way to get objective advice on the quality of that preparation and occasional advice on the ongoing quality of your work in search.

You can certainly have a successful search without a coach. Most job hunters do. And you can get much of the needed advice — and maybe all of it — from your Job Search Work Team or from individual team members. But still, a coach can be an asset.

If you decide to go this way, please carefully check a coach's background before spending money on them. Remember, this field is unregulated. There are no generally agreed upon or legally required qualifications. If someone you trust has already used their services, that's a great way to find out about them. But in any event, you should read their LinkedIn profile. If they don't have a good strong one, that's a red flag. They teach LinkedIn. They should know how to write a profile.

Do not ever, under any circumstances, pay a large lump sum to a coach. Most reputable coaches are available on an hourly basis. Many that ask for a lot of money and a signed contract have been found to be disreputable and even unethical.

If you're unemployed, and spending money on a career coach is not a good financial move for you, see if you can find a community program where career coaching is offered at no charge. Even in that case, I think you should read the coach's LinkedIn profile. But if there's no charge for the service, why wouldn't you try it?

2. Read several job hunting books, then use the Internet

Whether you have a coach or not and whether you're on a team or not, I think it's very important to read several job hunting books. Again, check the LinkedIn profiles of the authors. Look to see where they learned what they are now teaching.

You need a way to know that you are putting in enough effort every week

Do they have relevant experience? If so, how much? If their LinkedIn profile is heavy on trying to sell you things and light on the details of their experience, that's a red flag.

I recommend starting with books rather than the Internet. I've written––and read––material in both of those media, so I know the pros and cons of both. The reason I prefer books is that Internet job search information tends to be a fragmented collection of short articles on job hunting. It's often written by a number of unconnected authors, with little or no bio attached, so you don't know who's advising you.

But you can get books that zoom out for an overview of the whole project – or major parts of it – with a clearly identified author, one you can check on LinkedIn.

So I recommend using books to cover the initial skill topics, then using the Internet to go more deeply into some smaller pieces. So, for example, you might read a book on how to do networking in job search, then attend a webinar overview of LinkedIn, followed by some postings on how to use some of the most recent LinkedIn features.

On my website, www.highlyeffectivejobsearch.com, I've recommended some authors and books. But there are hundreds of others available as well.

These first two items, coaches and books, are mostly about the quality of your job search activities. As we've seen, the quantity of activity is also very important. Numerical tracking is mostly about quantity of activity. And a team is about both.

3. Use numerical progress tracking

I hope you will use numerical tracking, regardless of what else you do in your job search. The evidence is compelling that job hunters tend to do too little, and especially too little of the centrally important activities like networking. You need some reasonably objective way to know that you are putting in enough effort every week, week after week.

Numerical progress tracking can also provide some clues about quality of your search, since you can use them to see what's working for you and what's not.

4. Use a Job Search Work Team

A Job Search Work Team, of course, will support you in both the quality and quantity of your job search activities, from beginning to end.

I'm hoping that you'll be able to use the entire team process, because I know it works so well. If you know of a Job Search Work Team that you are definitely planning to join, then you're ready to get started right now. Or you can use the methods suggested for Adding New Members on page 43 as a way to find an existing team. And, of course, you can also ask around and search the Internet.

If you can't find a team that's convenient for you, you can start one. The best way to do that is to find one or two other job hunters who are also interested. Start by finding one other job hunter, using the Adding New Members approach. Then that person can help you find another. Once all three of you have read this book, you can get started having meetings while you are seeking additional members.

If you are a member of a religious community, you might ask a religious professional to assist you in getting a team started, and perhaps provide a meeting space. Teams operating inside of religious communities often add prayer or some other religious observance just before the meeting or just after it.

Or arrange some other regular, objective support for yourself

If you have read this entire book, you know enough to join a Job Search Work Team or to start one. But that doesn't mean that you have to. Thousands of people still find good jobs in more traditional ways, and you can too. While it might be the right decision to become a member of a team, it's also perfectly okay not to. Joining a team is not always practical. And there are other options.

One alternative is to locate one person who is willing to assist you. That person could be employed or not, a job hunter or not. It's better if they're not personally invested in your job search. So asking your spouse to do it is probably not a good idea.

Ask that person to read this book. Then the two of you should have regularly scheduled weekly meetings, on the phone or in person. The meetings will probably be 20 to 30 minutes in length. Agree on a time and stick with it. Use the JSWT numerical progress reporting and discussion format in an informal way.

But I hope you will use some kind of regular, objective support. It can go a long way to making things easier and faster.

That's it: Some books, maybe a coach, progress tracking, and some form of ongoing support, a JSWT or not. Those are the elements that you can use to put together your own job search program, one where you use a professional approach to the job search project.

So what's the next step for you?

Whatever you decide, may you find a great new job, one you really like.

May you find that job sooner than you think is possible.

And may you be happy and successful in that job for a good, long time.

A Note to Career Professionals

For much of my career, I have written for both job hunters and coaches, and this book is for both audiences, even though it's addressed to job hunters.

But this note is especially for program managers, career coaches and volunteer workers in career services programs. My purpose in writing it is to touch on those few topics relevant only to career professionals, and not to job hunters.

In this note, I'll focus particularly on the multi-team programs that career professionals often create. We'll also take a look at professional leadership, and maintaining the quality of JSWTs in larger programs.

Professional team leadership

One of the purposes of JSWTs is for diverse groups of job hunters to learn to find their own solutions to day-to-day job hunting problems, rather than being dependent on someone else for those solutions. As we all know, there is no single best way to handle many search–related activities. So advice from peers combined with professional assistance is an ideal combination.

A professional leader can best assist a JSWT advisory panel discussion by facilitating, rather than stepping in as an expert. And it's important that no leader, whether a professional or job hunter, uses more than their share of "air time" during the meeting. Any instructional assistance should be provided outside of the team meeting, as a separate event.

During team meetings, the professional leader should guide the group in the direction of increasing their expertise in job hunting, rather than providing that expertise for them. The occasional exceptions to this rule are those moments when a career coach can save the team, or an individual, significant time or effort by adding their observations to the group discussion or correcting misconceptions shared by the majority of the team. And having a career professional to lead the between-meeting activities listed in "Advanced Job Search Work Teams" is a significant advantage for job hunters.

When a professional team leader has already served as a counselor, coach or trainer for team members, the transition to team leader requires a bit of effort. Usually the most important part is acknowledging all useful contributions, with special attention to the best of them. And continually referring questions back to the team, rather than answering them.

And here's the most important point: By leading a Job Search Work Team, the career professional can easily see the individual job hunter's needs for counseling, coaching, or training, and therefore provide better, more focused services outside of the team meeting – while spending less time on the day-to-day job search coaching, task support and personal support that the team does so well.

Team leadership in multi-team programs

In a multi-team program, the teams can be led by professional leaders, volunteer workers, or the team members themselves. Even though there is a professional or volunteer leader, teams should elect leaders and alternates to lead the meeting when the regular leader is not available. When the professional team leader needs to miss a meeting, those internal member-leaders will usually do a better job of substituting for the regular leader than someone who has never worked with this particular team and doesn't know the team members.

No matter who the leaders are, it's a good idea to have a monthly leaders' meeting in any multi-team program. This is a great way to accelerate the learning of new team leaders and to maintain the overall quality of the program.

With member-led teams, those leaders' meetings can be scheduled as part of a monthly event for all participants in the job search assistance program. The monthly event might be a networking event, a workshop, or a speaker. I'm aware of a number of programs that use that structure, and it works well.

A monthly event for all program participants is also an opportunity for staff members and team members alike to recruit new members for the teams. Team members quickly notice that they need to fill the empty seat when someone lands a job. And that selecting the right person to fill the seat makes the team more effective for everyone.

Whether the teams are professionally led or member-led, the monthly leaders' meetings resemble Job Search Work Teams. Like the JSWTs, they begin with a brief report from each person. That report begins with job placements for the last month. If any Final Reports have been provided in writing, copies of them are collected by the program manager. With the permission of the authors, copies may also be distributed to all team leaders or shown to program funders.

The next item in the report is "highlights," the three things that are working best in the team. Finally, each leader in attendance may offer one or two agenda items. Like the JSWT agenda items, these are questions designed to elicit solutions to team leadership problems and ways to make the teams function better. Even with professional leaders, the answers to many of those questions can be found in this book.

Maintaining the quality of the teams

Those monthly leadership meetings are the single best way to maintain a high-quality team program, one that continues to produce a steady stream of job placements over time.

Another quality maintenance method involves team visits by the program manager. When doing these, be sure to tell the leader and team members a week in advance what's going to happen and why. The purpose, of course, is to make sure that the teams are working as well as possible, in order to get all of the members into great new jobs ASAP.

So make sure everyone knows at the outset that they will be receiving suggestions at the end of the meeting. And that any notes taken by the observer are not about particular people, but about how the team is functioning – and how it might function even better.

At the end of the meeting, the program manager should give feedback to the team. That feedback should not include any criticism. It should list three to six areas where the team is functioning well. And it should then provide two or three suggestions of how the team members can behave in even more productive ways – doing even more things that are likely to lead to more placements more quickly. These suggestions are often gentle reminders to more closely follow the instructions in this book.

After the meeting, in private, the program manager may give similar feedback to the team leader. Again, these are not criticisms. They are praise for success and suggestions on improved leadership behavior that will take the team to even higher levels of success.

Starting a new JSWT program

When adding Job Search Work Teams to an existing job search assistance program, it's particularly important that the first teams established include only the most committed and most competent job hunters.

Sometimes program managers want to start with the people who most need the help. But if that first team includes the least committed and the least competent job hunters, other job hunters might see the teams merely as a remedial program. With less committed members, the team would also be less likely to succeed. Then starting a second team could be difficult.

In fact, job hunters who are not clearly committed to success in job search probably shouldn't join the teams at all. I strongly recommend that participation in a JSWT program always be 100% voluntary. Prospective members should be required to read this book – and perhaps *The Unwritten Rules of the Highly Effective Job Search* as well — before visiting a team. This provides a test of commitment as well as preparation for immediate productivity on the team.

No one should ever pressure a prospective member to join a team. After all, someone who doesn't really want to be there is not likely to help make the team more productive – or to benefit very much from attendance. So please, invite, encourage and explain, but don't pressure anyone.

If you have questions, please e-mail me

I hope you found this book useful. I think that nonprofits, religious communities, government agencies and universities all face similar issues in providing high quality job search assistance services on limited budgets. I believe this book will make it easier for the leaders of any of those organizations to add Job Search Work Teams to their programs ––and enrich those programs without expanding their budgets.

If you have questions as you're getting started with a new multi-team program, I'd be happy to hear from you at Orville@highlyeffectivejobsearch.com. I'll respond as completely and as promptly as my schedule permits.

May Job Search Work Teams assist you in providing even better services to job hunters. May you see more and more people finding great new jobs faster.

Research Citations on Job Search Intensity

Studies show how the intensity of job search and the effort put into it are related to receiving more job offers and to having a shorter period of unemployment. Active job search intensity – as distinguished from intensity of preparatory activities – is strongly related to employment outcomes. However, intensity for unemployed job hunters tends to be low, ranging from 41 min/day (3.5 hrs/wk) to 3.5 hrs/day (17.5 hrs/wk).

"Temporal persistence," maintaining a reasonable job search intensity over the duration of a job search, is also shown to be important. The following studies deal with some or all of the above factors:

Wanberg CR, Zhu J, Van Hooft EAJ. 2010b. The job search grind: perceived progress, self reactions, and self-regulation of search effort. *Academy of Management Journal*. 53:788–807

Saks AM. 2006. Multiple predictors and criteria of job search success. *Journal of Vocational Behavior*. 68:400–15

Kanfer R, Wanberg CR, Kantrowitz TM. 2001. Job search and employment: a personality–motivational analysis and meta–analytic review. *Journal of Applied Psychology*. 86:837–55

Saks AM, Ashforth BE. 2000. Change in job search behaviors and employment outcomes. *Journal of Vocational Behavior*. 56:277–87

Kreuger AB, Mueller A. 2010. Job search and unemployment insurance: new evidence from time use data. *Journal of Public Economics*. 94:298–307

Research Citations on JSWT Effectiveness

Kondo, C. 2009. Benefits of job clubs for executive job seekers: a tale of hares and tortoises. *Journal of Employment Counseling*. Vol 46:27-37

Coxford, L, M, (1998), *The role of social support in the job-seeking behaviors of unemployed professionals*. Unpublished doctoral dissertation, Claremont Graduate University, Claremont, California,

Research Citations on Using a Job Search Workshop

JOBS, a 20-hour job search assistance workshop created at the University of Michigan, has been shown to be of real value in helping unemployed people find jobs. Among numerous other benefits were increased compensation, more positive states of mind and increased motivation. Here are two of the numerous citations on this program. Its curriculum is similar to the one in Chapter 7.

Price, R.H., & Vinokur, A.D. (1995). Supporting career transitions in time of organizational downsizing: the Michigan jobs program. In M. London (Ed.). *Employees, careers, and job creation: Developing growth-oriented human resource strategies and programs* (pp. 191-209). San Francisco: Jossey-Bass Publishers.

Vinokur, A.D., & Schul, Y. (1997). Mastery and inoculation against setbacks as active ingredients in the jobs intervention for the unemployed. *Journal of Consulting and Clinical Psychology*, 65, 867-877.

Acknowledgements

This book – and the Job Search Work Team process – is available to the general public through the generosity of Lee Hecht Harrison (LHH), the leading global career services firm. I'd particularly like to thank Steve Harrison, LHH's Co-founder and Chairman, for his support of Job Search Work Teams (JSWTs) — and me — from the day he agreed to hire me to the present day.

It was a great privilege to work with LHH's staff of career coaches for 19 years. It was part of my job to train them. But, in fact, I learned at least as much from them as they did from me. They are a highly experienced group, very smart, and devoted to great service for the clients they work with. Thanks to all of you for working with me over the years and sharing your wisdom on what works best in career and job search.

In particular, I'd like to thank the more than 300 coaches who successfully completed the grueling JSWT leadership certification process that I insisted on. And I'd like to thank everyone I worked with at LHH over the years. I learned so much from you all, and you'll see some of it in this book.

A number of current and former LHHers — and a few who never worked there — provided significant assistance with this book. This group has a total of over 200 years experience in career work and over a century's experience with JSWTs. Included in this group are some of the very best career professionals available. It was a privilege to have their assistance.

Thank you to Andrew Johnson, Bill Thomas, Cheryl Greenhalgh, Claudia Gentner, Cori Ashworth, Deb Krawiec, Ed DeVries, Ed McEneney, Grace Totoro, Jay Colan, Jean Baur, Jess Dods, Joe Ciola, Randy Ruppart, Rick Hays and Rosemary Monahan.

I'm also indebted to four PhD's, all with university experience, for their generous assistance with the research I included in this book. I'd particularly like to thank Dr. Connie Wanberg, Professor of Industrial Relations at the University of Minnesota, for helping me locate – and better understand – relevant research on job search. Thanks also to Drs. Amiram Vinokur, Chris Kondo, and Kathryn Tracy for information and assistance with research.

Once again, I'd like to thank my writing coach, Peter Sugarman, who worked with me on this book, as he did on my two previous books. Thanks, Peter, for helping me make it clearer, simpler and more pleasant to read. Thanks to Susan Bassett, my creative partner for many years at LHH, for her suggestions, especially for the book's concluding elements. Thanks to Keith Owens, who made extensive editorial suggestions as well as several useful content suggestions. And thanks to Becky Brillon and Shelley Rieger for their editorial comments.

So many people were so helpful with this book that I'm quite concerned that I have failed to mention someone. If that's you, thank you. Please send me a reminder, and I'll do what I can to make amends for omitting your name.

Now I want to thank the most important people in my life, my family. They are such lovely people! I'm so glad to be related to them! And they helped me with all my books, including this one.

Thanks to my daughter, Sarah Beaulieu, for her usual incisive comments, made even though she was busy with job and family. And many thanks to my son Paul, for outstanding content suggestions that produced a major new section of the book, as well as for his expert assistance with graphic design and other aspects of completing this project.

I find it difficult to thank my wife, Judy, for all that she's done, because words seem inadequate. But quite simply, without her, this book would not have been written.

My dear, dear Ramala, it's your love and support over the years that have enabled me to grow to the point where I could write books that people find useful. For nearly forty years, you've been an enormous force for good in my life — and supportive of my work as well. Thank you for repeatedly reading and commenting on this book. Thank you for everything.

Finally, I want to acknowledge the great teachers and saints who offer us guidance in everything in life and bring us daily closer to God. And I acknowledge God's grace, active in this book as it is in everything, everywhere, always. Thank you, Lord.

Other Books by Orville Pierson

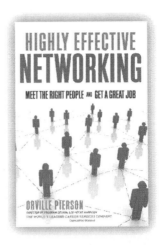

The Unwritten Rules of the Highly Effective Job Search:
The Proven Program Used by the World's Leading Career Services Company

Published by McGraw-Hill

This book is about planning and managing a job search in ways that are much more effective than those traditionally used by job hunters. It includes four chapters on the job search Project Plan and one on the Target List, as well as extensive information on reality-checking your planning, using numerical progress measurements and other aspects of highly effective job hunting.

Highly Effective Networking:
Meet the Right People and Get a Great Job

Published by Career Press

Job search networking is the most misunderstood and most abused part of job hunting. This book provides a common-sense approach, based on years of experience of what actually works in job search – and what job hunters are comfortable doing. The book empowers you to:

- Use even a small network to reach dozens of insiders and Decision Makers

- Get the right message to the right people, even if you never met them

- Speak effectively and comfortably with your networking contacts

- Talk to Decision Makers before the job opening is announced

- Use social networking websites to support making the personal contacts that are essential to success

---